All In God's Time, My Sons

Poems and reflections on the deaths of Andrew and Matthew Moeller by their father,

Geoff Moeller

2010

ireadiwrite Publishing Edition

Copyright © 2010 Geoff Moeller

This ireadiwrite Publishing edition is published by arrangement with Geoff Moeller, contact at arcticborn@hotmail.com

ireadiwrite Publishing -www.ireadiwrite.com

First print edition published by ireadiwrite Publishing

All In God's Time, My Sons

ISBN 978-1-926760-31-5

Published in Canada with international distribution.

Cover Design: Michelle Halket
Cover Photograph: Copyright Geoff Moeller

"Many people have written about death and radical injustice and what happens to us when tragedy strikes. Many have written moving poems about these subjects, some have composed profound theological or psychological reflections about the process of grieving and loss. But in this extraordinary collection of poems by Geoff Moeller there is something more and greater. Here the heart of a father is laid bare as he lives with the stark reality of the death of his two sons, as well as the paralysis of his surviving son, and the grievous wounds suffered by his whole family. In this most moving and beautiful book you will find true faith--the kind that is tested in fire--the faith that is a resounding affirmation of life. It is a story that cracks open our hearts. It makes us see with new eyes, and helps us to treasure the gifts that are given to us, which we so often take for granted."

—Michael D. O'Brien

Author of *Father Elijah, An Apocalypse* and *Island of the World*

FOREWORD

I thank Geoff for the privilege of writing the Foreword to this inspiring and unique collection of poems. It has been my pleasure to have known Geoff since 1989 and Maria since 1990 when Geoff introduced me to his beautiful new girlfriend. Having officiated at their wedding (what I like to call "the birthday of their family") in 1994, I have journeyed with this family through the years...years which saw an increasingly bouncy and vibrant family life emerge with the births of their four sons. The youngest, Lorenzo, I am proud to call my Godson. No one could have imagined that on November 29, 2008, a new reality would dramatically overwhelm their world. Every aspect of their being...heart, mind, body and soul...was challenged. Many at the time wrote or asked, "Where is God in all this?" I observed how God was truly present in the immediate and compassionate outpouring of prayers and support from so many people, both friends and strangers, locally, nationally and abroad. God was present in the inspiring arrangements of the funeral for their sons, A.J. and Matthew, in which Geoff and Maria strove so courageously to bring comfort to others. Comfort...in the truest sense...con+fortis which literally means with strength! God is indeed very much present in the message of love and inspiration coming forth from these poems. In the reading of them we all are raised up and blessed.

This collection of poetry comes from a heart that ponders. Geoff makes very real for me what Our Blessed Mother Mary presents to us in Scripture - what it truly means to ponder. Mary pondered these things in her heart (Lk. 2) How did Mary ponder? She was peacefully present to the reality around her. Her reality had much that was confusing, puzzling, troubling, dark and deathly for her. Her reality very much pierced her heart where it met God, her Saviour. There she pondered her reality. Forth from her pondering heart flowed that which was loving, clear, peaceful, joyful, strong (truly "comforting"), hope-filled, positive, upward-attentive and centred on Divine Providence. Her Magnificat is poetry from a heart that ponders. "My soul magnifies the Lord, my spirit rejoices in God, my Saviour." (Lk. 1)

In this collection of poems Geoff shares with us the fruits of a pondering heart, one that has witnessed the transforming power of God in the midst of a troubling, piercing reality. What flows forth is a light which dispels darkness, a strength which is truly a source of comfort, a message of faith and hope which is a beacon for all those weighed down by realities of darkness, confusion and fear. It is a beautiful legacy for their sons, Karl and Lorenzo, and all who will read these poems. What flows forth is Geoff's Magnificat!

Fr. Ian Charles Stuart
Solemnity of Mary, Mother of God
January 1, 2010

Andrew Joseph Moeller

June 3, 1999 – November 29, 2008
Taken at: Disneyland, September 2008

Matthew Benedict Moeller

March 18, 2002 – November 29, 2008

Taken at Jones Park, 2008

All In God's Time,
My Sons

Poems and reflections on the deaths of Andrew and
Matthew Moeller by their father, Geoff Moeller

The Accident

On Saturday, November 29, 2008 around 9AM, the vehicle holding my wife Maria, my four sons Andrew, Karl, Matthew and Lorenzo, my mother-in-law Rita, her sister Pas and Pas' daughter Marlene was struck from behind by a SUV. My wife had stopped due to mechanical trouble. The SUV, traveling at freeway speed and swerving into the HOV lane, collided full-force into the rear of the minivan carrying my family.

Karl, Andrew and Matthew sat in the rear seats, right-to-left.

Karl suffered a spinal cord injury causing paralysis below the chest, a laceration to the back of his head, a broken femur on one leg and a broken tibia on the other. His paralysis is permanent.

Andrew suffered massive trauma to his head, and irreparable damage to his brain. Andrew's time of death was officially 9PM that night.

Matthew suffered a broken neck. It took thirty minutes to get his heart working again, but the lack of oxygen did irreparable damage to his brain and heart. Matthew's time of death was officially 9PM that night.

Pas, Rita and Lorenzo sat in the middle seats, right-to-left.

Pas suffered a spinal injury, broken pelvis and a head injury. She has been released from hospital.

Rita suffered a spinal injury requiring surgery. She has been released from hospital.

Lorenzo suffered only a minor bruise on one thigh from his car seat seatbelt.

Marlene sat in the passenger seat. She suffered whiplash to her neck.

Maria was driving. She suffered minor impacts to her leg, a facial abrasion and ongoing emotional trauma.

The other driver was uninjured.

I was at work when I received the phone call from my wife in the hospital.

As though the accident, the deaths of Andrew and Matthew, and the injuries to those in the minivan were not enough to deal with, my wife and I also encountered overwhelming media attention during our time of grief. Maria and I soon realized the deaths of Andrew and Matthew, and Karl's paralysis, too, had affected a vast number of people, that number growing each day, beyond the effect on just our little family. It became evident God was working on peoples' hearts, the accident becoming a source of grace to guide the thoughts of many to Him. Observing the workings of grace strengthened my faith and helped me to recognize a greater meaning in the tragedy.

Over the days and months that followed, I found comfort in writing. At times, it seemed a battle waged between faith and emotion, but, the more I wrote, the more I realized the battle had more to do with each needing balanced expression; clinging only to faith denied my humanity, while focusing too much on loss and grief tended toward self-pity and the denial of faith and hope in God's promises.
I wrote (and write still) because I needed to for myself. Gradually, as more people began to read my poems and reflections, they suggested I publish them for others experiencing similar tragedies, or for someone who could possibly find comfort in them. In the pages that follow are the public statements released after the accident and all the poems and reflections written after the deaths of my much-missed sons Andrew and Matthew.

Prayer as My Family Slept

(written in early November 2008, before the accident)

Dear Lord, my sons sleep peacefully,
What riches in each boy given me!
But, oh, the moments go so fast!
I can't undo mistakes of the past,
but resolve in the music of their breathing
To rejoice in the wonder of each son's being.

Stoop down, majestic angels, and see,
The divinity God has shared with me!
Embodied souls, my precious sons,
Worth more than planets, stars or suns,
Called to be, to live eternally,
Lie here entrusted, unworthily, to me.

Make up, dear Lord, for my weakness.
Replace impatience with Your meekness.
Open my arms to give affection,
And guide my mind to give direction.
May Your grace so live in me
That my sons may grow to see
The loving God You are, and they
Will choose to follow You and pray
For grace and strength to do Your will,
That Your plan for them might be fulfilled.

With a father's right, I claim before You now,
Through the sign of Jesus on each brow,
Every blessing conceived in Your paternal love.
Through the power of the Spirit send from above
The graces my sons shall need to be
Men of faith, of love, and sanctity.

Holy Virgin, unfailing refuge in my life,
I entrust to you my children and my wife.
Guard them better than I ever could.
Love them stronger than I ever would.
I have asked – it shall be done
For the glory of the Father through the merits of the Son.
Amen.

Media Release
December 4, 2008

On behalf of my wife, children and family, I'd like to express my deepest appreciation for all the good wishes and prayers for us from so many people. Nothing I could say or do could adequately express my admiration and gratitude to the first responders at the scene of the accident, the doctors and nurses at both Royal Columbia and BC Children's Hospitals for every effort made to care for my wife, sons and relatives. The respect and tenderness shown to Andrew and Matthew even after their deaths moved me deeply and was a great comfort to my wife and me. Thank-you, too, to the priests who anointed and blessed my sons. Our faith has strengthened and consoled my wife and me for the loss of our dear boys Andrew and Matthew, and has helped us to be strong for our surviving boys Lorenzo and Karl, who continues to recover with the loving care of the nurses in the ICU in Children's Hospital. Please continue to pray for my mother-in-law and her sister in critical condition in Royal Columbia Hospital.

Andrew and Matthew are gone, but just from our sight. One day, with God's grace, I hope to be with them again.

Thank-you and God bless.

Eulogy
December 9, 2008

It's the call no father wants to hear.

It's the call no mother wants to make.

The deaths of AJ and Matthew would be unacceptable, unbearable if not for faith telling me our children are more alive now than just ten days ago; if not for hope urging me on to see AJ and Matthew in heaven; if not for love which flowed from them, from all of you, and from God.

God's love poured from the hearts of every person rushing to the accident scene, from every doctor and nurse leaning over our boys' injured bodies, from every friend and relative hearing the awful news, from every stranger moved by the simple truth that the loss of AJ and Matthew affects us all.

Mayet and I have the joy and honour of being the parents of AJ and Matthew, but you who are relatives, you who are priests and teachers, you who are friends... in so far as you gave part of yourself and became part of AJ and Matthew, you became part of our family. Recognizing this is a blessing the Father gives us in our sorrow – we are family.

Mayet and I have been overwhelmed by the outpouring of love, prayer and generosity from family, friends, co-workers, and people we don't even know. Please accept our undying gratitude. We have been truly humbled by the gifts and help given so freely and unselfishly. We owe a great debt of gratitude to Ocean View Burial Park for covering the funeral expenses for our sons. Thank-you to Gigi, Fr. Ian, Glicer, Aunt Emma, the teachers and students of St. Francis of Assisi School, Fr. Bede, Fr. Michael, and all who helped in any way organizing and preparing this beautiful liturgy. Thank-you all for coming to celebrate our belief that AJ and Matthew are alive in God and will be reunited with their bodies freed from all suffering when the Lord raises them.

It wasn't enough for AJ to care about children and the poor, he had to express his compassion by his actions. Just a few weeks ago I showed him a news clipping about starving children. That night he had me print it from the computer, and the next day he made a presentation to his class with a tin can from home. The money collected was to be sent before Christmas. I understand that his class will finish this project in his name.

Matthew could warm any gathering with his smile. On the days when I took him for a treat and he could choose where he wanted to go, he would choose a certain fast food place with a play area so he could play with the children there. On the way home he would say something like, "I made three friends today."

All who knew AJ and Matthew loved them. The people gathered in this church are reflections and expressions of that love. The recipients of their organs share in that love and pass it on to the people in their lives. Only God could bring such beauty and grace from such pain and anguish.

How God has comforted Mayet and me. AJ and Matthew were anointed not once, but three times by different priests. Another confirmed them, and two more blessed them. Six priests were sent by the Lord more for our sake than for AJ and Matthew. It's as though the Lord were saying, "What can I do to make it clear these children are with Me?" I wondered why AJ and Matthew should need Confirmation, but I realized once again the Lord was showing us they had reached the fullness of faith, had in fact passed beyond faith because they see God face to face and plead for us with the persistent innocence of children saying to God the Father, "Did you answer my prayer yet? Did you answer my prayer yet?"

I'm so proud of you, AJ. I'll try to learn from your example. Mommy and I love you so much. Matthew, your smile must be making the angels sing. Mommy and I love you and miss you both.

My boys, pray for Karl to get well, and for Mama and Mama Nene, too. Pray for us that one day we will join you in heaven.

Amen.

The Funeral Homily by Abbot John Braganza OSB (Order of Saint Benedict)

December 10, 2008

The gift of children and the loss of children. These are the two mysteries of life God asks us to ponder today. They are mysteries in the conventional sense – things hard to understand – and in a special sense – with reference to Jesus Christ their meaning changes.

For society in general, today the gift of children is difficult to accept. We adults can be so intent on our own rights and pleasures, our own personal happiness that we can think of our children as a problem. Indeed, for very many, the child is a disease to be rid of before birth.

Again for society at large, the loss of children is too hard to bear. Where God is not the source and center of our life and our children, then we can cling to them as though we were the author of their lives and as if we had a right of possession over them. Their loss becomes altogether insupportable.

Today, the tragic death of these two you boys can help us discover the gift of God in our loss and the greater gift behind the gift they were to us. We need to discover again the Christian meaning of the gift and the loss.

Our first reading is gentle in its application to the lives of these two boys. In a way the intention of the parents are expressed – that their children belong to God first and then to them. Samuel's mother gave Samuel to God soon after he was weaned – perhaps at three or four years of age. Children are never too young for God – we adults put these limitations on them.

Like Samuel, both Andrew and Matthew served in the Temple of God, in this Church as altar boys. Fr. Bede tells me Andrew burnt his finger the day of the accident. Thinking of Jesus' gentleness with children, I see in that incident Our heavenly Father preparing little Andrew for his great encounter with Him.

Every little wound is a foreshadowing of our death. This was perhaps the first gentle summons. We should not underestimate a child's capacity to face its own death with greater serenity than adults because they receive life as a gift.

Let us not hesitate to think that these two young lads embraced their death with the same love as they embraced life. Look at the young Samuel. Who would not wish one's son this great openness to God:

"Speak Lord, your servant is listening."

In death our ears and our hearts are totally open. All that Geoff and Mayet taught them, they would have brought with great simplicity to that solemn hour.

The Gospel reading too, is especially appropriate, both for them and for us who mourn. For them because we know they knew Jesus in Baptism, Confession, Holy Communion and the last anointing. In each of those sacraments Jesus revealed the face of his Father to them.

For us – Jesus says – "Don't separate your two sons' death from my death – only in my death do their deaths find meaning. Above all do not separate your sorrow from me – mourn in me and the burden of your sorrow will be easy and light for you.

So St. Paul reminds us: "do not grieve about those who have died, like other people who have no hope."

Allow me to share one last thought: All who have died in Jesus live in Jesus. In Jesus we all form one Body. Do not grieve overmuch but think that daily, even today, you can meet your sons in the Holy Eucharist. Are they not with Jesus? Is Jesus not present in the Eucharist? In the days ahead when you long for them remember how close they really are!

The solution to the mystery of the gift of children and the loss of children can be found only in Jesus – in his gift to us – in the Eucharist which is both the gift of his life and his death and resurrection.

Letter to the Editor of the BC Catholic
Published January 13, 2009

So many people have reached out to my wife, Maria, and me since the accident which caused the death of our sons Andrew and Matthew and injured our son Karl and my mother-in-law, Rita, and her sister, Pas. I would like to publicly express our heartfelt appreciation and gratitude to all.

Many have asked me how I can bear such a tragedy, how I can be strong after losing two sons on the same day. The following lines are meant to reveal my attitude and beliefs, and also witness to the blessings I believe God has given through this accident.

On the mantle at home stand portraits of Andrew and Matthew. Their eyes stare through me and my heart aches knowing I will not see them alive again in this world. Yet, at the moment when I could succumb to an immense wave of grief, I sense Andrew and Matthew nearby. They put the choice before me: cling to memories of them as they were, or love them as they are now, saints in heaven with God.

I miss their hugs, smiles, voices, laughter, the way they sleep, the way they look... however, I would not ask God to give them back to me because they have reached the goal I had in mind for them on the day they were born – heaven!

Rather than me dying before them, though, God has decided it's better they should go first. Andrew and Matthew call to me every day to live a life of readiness and to learn from their sudden death. Time and life are not to be taken for granted. Andrew and Matthew are such blessings in my life. Now they are blessings for the Church and the world, too.

On Friday, Dec. 5, during a Mass offered for Karl, Rita and Pas, I sensed Andrew and Matthew beside me, and they were so happy. They thanked me for their baptism and for being raised in the Faith, and that is why I have not been too sad since they died.

Yes, the accident was horrendous and caused much pain and anguish, but God salvaged much good from the wreckage. There are two new saints in heaven, eight people are alive through organ donation, family relationships have been strengthened, the parish and school communities at St. Francis of Assisi and others have become closer, and the general public have opened their hearts in love and witnessed faith in response to this accident.

The funeral Mass for Andrew and Matthew Dec. 10 was one of the most beautiful liturgical celebrations I have ever attended. The caskets containing the bodies of my sons lay like reliquaries before the altar. Father Abbot John Braganza delivered an inspired and comforting homily, and later sang the Te Deum* with Brothers Maximus and Gabriel. The Te Deum! For my sons, and sung by an abbot!

Father Bede said it well at the end of Mass: not even dignitaries have the Te Deum sung at their funerals. The funeral of Andrew and Matthew was a celebration of the hope we have of eternal life with God. They have reached that goal. Every day I want to make heaven my goal, too, since that is the only way I'll ever get to see Andrew and Matthew again.

* The Te Deum is a Latin hymn of praise usually sung at the conclusion of a joyous liturgical occasion such as a special feast day. The first words of the hymn are Te Deum laudamus (We praise You, O God).

Communion, A Meditation

They had been there for hours. The fire had burnt the last branch and bit of animal flesh. The warm glow from the seething embers cast flickering shadows on their faces, their minds deep in thought. Stillness hung in the night air, a waiting hopefulness like the moments after a great event, for such had happened in this rocky outcrop. Stars sparkled mutely like children waiting to be born.

Sitting at the edge of the darkness, I watched them, the old, old man, and the boy at the cusp of manhood. The elder rocked gently on his seat, a rock put there for him by the boy. He held his upturned palms before his bearded face, his eyes closed, though tears never ceased flowing, his mouth moaning words with barely audible sounds. Sighs shuddered his thin frame from time to time, then gasps of joy when he seemed to glow brighter than the red hot coals. At these sounds, the boy poked his stick into the coals, his blazing eyes staring at a large knife lying on another stone before the makeshift pyre, the dull red glow reflected on its curved metal blade. He looked up, straight into my eyes.

"You're wondering why I didn't try to run," he said, in a way demanding an answer.

I nodded slowly, amazed at his composure.

He continued stabbing at the coals as he talked. "My earliest memories are of my mother telling me the story of how the Lord God visited the home of my parents, promising them a son in spite of their old age, and how I am their miracle child. I heard what happened to my aunt when she looked back at Sodom. I've seen the faith of my father blessed countless times. Who am I to question the will of God?" He paused, an anguished look crossing his face like a storm cloud over the smooth sands of the desert.

"Yes?" I asked, quietly encouraging him.

The look faded and he met my gaze again. "I saw the look in my father's eyes after we built the pyre. I knew then what was going to happen. There was a moment, the briefest tremble when I wanted to run away screaming: No, I want to live! But I love my father more than my own life and to take away his pain at what the Lord was asking him to do, I willingly lay on the branches. I resigned myself to the will of the Lord; after all, He gave me to my father; surely He had the right to take me back again." He turned at the sound of the old man struggling to his feet, his blue-veined hands grasping a well-polished staff. The boy was at his side instantly, his arms wrapped tightly around him, supporting him. The old man released the staff and raised his tear-stained face to heaven, his arms extended. His rich voice filled the silent sky with praise.

"Blessed are You, Lord of Life,
Who gives life and Who takes life;
Blessed are You, Lord God of all creation,
For there is no other in all the universe
Deserving of praise and adoration."

Gazing down at his son embracing him, he continued,

"I thank-you, Lord, for this son of mine,
This fulfillment of Your promise,
Received first in joy as a mere babe;
Received now as born through a testing fire.
Praise and glory to You Lord God
Who rewarded the steadfast faith of Your servant

And blessed the sacrificial love of Your servant's son!
Neither life nor death shall turn us from You,
For there is no other;
You are God.
Amen and amen."

Abraham motioned to the ground, and together father and son lay prostrate before the consumed pyre, with only the ram's horned skull remaining in the coals, their hands stretched out before them, their faces in the dust. I, too, fell to the ground, as much by the power of their devotion as by the reality of the presence of the God of Abraham, the God of Isaac, and, by the death of His Son Jesus unknown to Abraham in his time, my God, too.

The coals of the pyre lay cold and black as the dawning sun pushed back the night. I awoke to see Abraham seated on his rock and studying me. Isaac bent over a fire a short distance away, The smell of cooked meat made my stomach growl.

"Good morning, son," said my father in faith. The emotion of the previous day had passed. His dark eyes, though kindly, peered at me intently. He seemed excited as he twisted the ends of his long white beard. His breathing quickened, his eyes grew wide. "What is He like, son?" Abraham asked, leaning forward with eyes glistening.

"Who, Father Abraham?"

"The Promised One, my distant descendant for Whom all this was made and by Whom it shall be won back to God," he said, casting an arm across the shining morning sky, the other grasping his staff. "What is He like?" he repeated eagerly.

"How could you know of Him, Father?" I asked, amazed at the soul of this man.

"The Lord my God is more necessary to me than the air I breathe," Abraham intoned, eyes closed, face raised to heaven. Looking at me once more, he continued, "I hear truths echo in the innermost corners of my soul and collect them greedily as a sparrow gathers crumbs. Of He-Who-Is-To-Come, I could glean His coming only through the faith given me from God. For what other purpose should Almighty God speak to dust like me and make promises of my offspring? Whether you are here present to me, or I to you, through the power of God, it is of little consequence; here you are, a witness to the fact of His coming in the fullness of God's Plan. Is this not true faith: knowing something to be true even unseen? He is to come, yet He lives in you! My heart bursts at His presence – yes, Lord, (my son!) live in me, too! For this world... my faith... nothing would exist if not for You. O let me die in the assurance of my faith! Remove the remaining fog of this life that I might see my God face-to-face!"

How weak was my poor faith beside this greatest of patriarchs! How many times had I received the Lord carelessly in Holy Communion, and taken His Passion and Death for granted in Confession? Shame covered me.

"There is something else I must say, my son," Abraham said, motioning me near. Placing his staff on the ground beside him, he took my hand in both of his, drawing me down to sit before him. I was surprised by his strength and the compassion in his eyes. "The Lord has given me an insight into your pain. Perhaps that is why He has permitted you to be here. The Lord's angel did not hold back the crashing metal of your sons' deaths because they lived in faith – they knew His Son and lived in Him. It was a far greater gift to take them to Himself than to permit them to live in a world which may have led them away from Him; is it not so? The gift of their passing was meant not only for them but for you and your community that the true purpose of this life be always before your souls. Their deaths stand as long as you live as a guidepost on the way to God." He sighed, gazing far over the hills. "My son and I stand at the dawning of God's revealing Himself to man," he said, nodding slowly as his eyes rested on me again.

There was wonder in his voice. "You, my son, stand near the consummation! All these tests are part of His Plan. He created us without our help, but He asks our help to bring about His Plan of Salvation. Do you understand?"

I nodded, tears streaming down my face that he should be aware of my sons' deaths, and that they should have such an important part to play in the salvation of souls. But then I realized Abraham and Isaac of course would know of my sons' deaths, belonging as they do to the Communion of Saints. Isaac's voice interrupted my thoughts.

"You must be hungry, brother. Have some meat; here are bread and wine, too," he smiled, a large platter in his hands.

In that instant, I was alone once more, the Book of Genesis open on the table before me, a cool breeze rattling the blinds against the open window, and the sounds of sirens and honking cars on the streets outside.

Lejac Pilgrimage in Honour of Rose Prince
July 10-12, 2009

My wife Maria and I joined the candlelight procession and stood beside the grave of Rose Prince with hundreds of others. Would our son Karl receive a miracle through her prayers and be healed? We dearly wanted him to walk again. The many testimonies of healing and graces received strengthened our respect and devotion toward our new friend in heaven.

On the long drive north from Vancouver to the beautiful pilgrimage site on an open field overlooking Fraser Lake, I asked the Lord to heal Karl's spinal cord injury. I bargained with God: heal Karl and my life is yours to use as You see fit! I tried to pretend I didn't recall the bible verse that said my life had already been bought and paid for by the sacrifice of Jesus and I was to live for Him anyway, miracle or no miracle! Yet, I still pleaded: Son of David, have mercy on us! Why should Karl have to bear this injury? Isn't it enough that he has to live with the loss of his brothers Andrew and Matthew?

Over the course of the three-day pilgrimage, my wife and I also took Karl and Lorenzo to play at the beach and sight-see. Karl seemed accepting of his situation and laughed easily. He rarely complained about being unable to walk. I realized that Karl was showing an accepting spirit, living according to what he could do, and not according to what he could not. Most of the time, things he wanted to do were not impossible, they just required a little more effort! Was it Karl who needed a miracle, or me? Why was it so necessary to me that Karl walk again? Did I think less of him? Of course not; the reason lay more in letting go of my pride in the four healthy sons I had had; I needed to rejoice in the living miracle of Karl as he was now. I also began to realize how the Lord was giving Maria and me opportunities to grow closer to Karl by performing the special care he needed. Maria would gently roll him onto his side when he needed help with his hygiene, and I would carry him from his wheelchair to the beach or lift him to places he couldn't go by himself. Karl is more gentle, more compassionate now. I believe living through his injury, seeing other, smaller children in hospital, often with more serious ailments, has greatly affected him. He shares a tragic bond with his mother and little brother from the accident, and they are much closer to each other because of it, sharing a heightened love for life, primarily through family. Maria confided in me that she began the pilgrimage for Karl's sake, but had received healing graces for her own heart.

Each day is full of miracles, for each grace is a miracle. The grace to accept and be thankful to the Lord for what, and most especially who, he gives us each day is one miracle for which I praise Him. Maria and I continue to ask Rose Prince to pray that Karl may walk again, and we use soil from her grave site mixed with holy water on his back. Rose Prince of the Carrier Nation, pray for us!

All In God's Time,
My Sons

Falling on their caskets in my mind

I cast my senses into the flames
For I shall not use them here again
To touch, to hear, to smell their bodies
Playfully muddied or freshly washed,
Save only upon death's silken pillows.
I cling instead to my cold, cold faith
And lay my tortured raging heart
Before Your altar of sacrifice
And the coffins of my sons.

*D*oes faith hold back my tears?

Let me put away my shield of faith;
Let me but for one moment lay
The armor of God's grace aside
That my eyes could shed oceans of grief,
My lungs unleash such anguished howls
That clinging to the portraits of my car-killed sons,
I could mourn with groans from my very soul.

The world is changed forever

The world smiles and goes its merry way -
STOP!
My sons have died.
The world has no right
To act as though it has not been wounded, too.

for Matthew

Matthew smiled and I smiled, too;
He called me 'Da-ee' when just two.
He snuggled with Mommy after prayers,
His Pokemon pillow went everywhere.
He rode on my shoulders to go to school,
Liked video games – Sonic was 'cool'.
He laughed with AJ reading his books,
Liked playing chess with bishops and rooks.
He liked apples, peeled, sliced and cored,
Treats with Mommy bought at a store,
Vanilla ice cream in a cone or a bowl,
Rolling with his brothers down grassy knolls.
He tickled Lorenzo and loved him, too,
Loved wild animals and trips to the zoo.
He played checkers with Karl and liked to draw,
Had the brightest smile I ever saw.

I miss you, Matthew, and your little-boy laugh;
Why did God take you at six-and-a-half?

$\mathcal{M}$eeting my boys in prayer

Reach down from your place of rest, my sons,
For I cannot go where you have gone.
Part the veil that hides you from my sight
In the timeless now beyond this light.
Clasp your gentle souls with mine outstretched
And draw me from this world so wretched
Where sons can die with lives barely granted,
Yet be laid to rest with love like seeds of love planted.
And, watered with my tears, my heart becomes love's earth
From which blooms wisdom: the precious worth
Of life, of time, of each new neighbour
Who meets me needy or helpful in my labour;
He is Christ to me as I ought be to him.
Oh, let me learn from your short life's hymn;
Your deaths, though sudden, found you both prepared.
If God called me to judgment, would I be spared?
Andrew and Matthew, pray for my soul,
And help us, your family, make heaven our goal.

Looking for strength

Within my canyoned heart
I drink from the rock of Christ;
Cupped hands, trembling at my lips,
Collect my chaliced tears
Co-mingling with the tears of Him
Who wept at the death of His friend.
Does He weep for my sons, too?
Or, rather, does He weep for me?
For my boys are with Him now -
Thank God for the gift of Faith!
I submit my emptied palms
To this crucifying sadness,
For only from the vantage of the cross
Can I glimpse the distant Resurrection.

for AJ

Oh, first-born, longed-for, gentle son,
Do you remember riding on my back at one?
Or sitting in my lap to hear a story?
Or sleeping on my chest as I sat snoring?
Oh, responsible, caring oldest brother,
Pride and joy of your loving mother,
So protective of Karl when you were four,
And good with Matthew in the store,
How you loved Lorenzo, too,
I wish he could have grown with you.
I miss you, AJ (Andrew Joseph),
Even though I'm sure you know it.
My heart feels close to breaking
When I think that you were aching
At anything I'd done and not said sorry,
Or not taken time to hear your story.
And now, my son, I can't even hold you,
And wonder if I ever really told you
How proud you made me many times.
"I love you, Daddy." rang like chimes.
I loved to see you hold your candle
Serving at the altar, and how you handled
Yourself playing sports and at school,
How you followed the Golden Rule.
Now, each day, I long to see you again,
Hear you, hold you, tell you again
The things a father thinks, but sometimes waits;
And now, for me, it is too late,
Except before your portrait on the mantle,
Or in my heart while lighting a candle.
Oh, my son, I know you hear me,
And how I need to believe you're near me!
Turn these tears of mine to rhymes
To honor you and all the times
We had together though far too brief.

Give me love to heal my grief,
And in memory of you and Matthew,
I'll be a better father, my dear son, Andrew.

$\mathcal{A}$lone at home in the silence

Oh burning, burning gaze
Across the widening days,
Never let this aching mend
Nor let it fail to rend
The promise of the world,
Nor pry my fingers curled
And grasping all but God.
Your deaths shall be His rod
Smashing all illusions,
Guiding past delusions;
For life is God's free gift,
The means to cross the rift,
And time is but the test
Meriting true rest.
Until then your youthful eyes
From portraits cry, "Be wise!"
And brim with silent love
To draw my thoughts above.

for Enzo

Come, Lorenzo, play with me
With choo-choo trains and building blocks
and storybooks read
With you sitting on my knee.

Come, Lorenzo, let me see
Your tousled hair and chubby cheeks,
and fingernails clipped
With you sitting on my knee.

Come, Lorenzo, pray with me
At supper time and sleepy time,
and Mass time spent
With you sitting on my knee.

Come, Lorenzo, be with me
At AJ's grave and Matthew's grave,
and thanking God for Karl
With you standing at my knee.

Come, Lorenzo, stay with me
For toddler days and high school days,
and grown-up days prayed
With me falling to my knees.

for Karl

The bright pink scar along your spine
Has marked you, precious son of mine,
As one who suffered, yet survived!
Live not in pity nor feel deprived,
But breathe each day's blessings in,
And with your own great efforts win
The self-respect and pride in you
That grows with each good thing you do.
Could I have known the simple worth
Of giving you your name at birth?
For you are Karl – man of strength -
And, guided by your patron saints,
You'll overcome this injury
And mark your life with victory!
And, as the days and years go by,
You shall also learn to fly
By setting goals in life and love
While trusting in the Lord above.

Staring from a coffee shop window in late winter

melting snows
bright sun crocus colours
open jackets
arm-in-arm warm smiles
cracked pavement
potholes jarred memories
marble crypt
tear-stained December
changing seasons
your absence heartache

Seeing past the pain

What is it like in heaven, sons,
How wonderful is the Lord?
Does Mother Mary mother you,
St. Michael show his sword?
Do choirs of angels sing for you,
The saints all gather round?
Did you tug on Moses' beard,
Wrestle Jacob to the ground?
Has John the Baptist winked and said
That locusts are good to eat,
And did you meet St. Joseph yet,
Then sit quietly at his feet?
Did Fr. Ponti tap your head
Like when he saw you after Mass,
Or did he simply welcome you with:
"You made it home at last!"
Do you shout across the universe
And scream with sheer delight
At all that lies before your eyes
Resplendent in the Father's light?
Do you gaze at God then turn away
Just so you can look again?
And each time seeing something new,
You praise, then praise again?
Have you scouted unseen galaxies,
Or walked on Saturn's rings?
Have you pulled at strands of DNA,
Unravelled hidden things?
Are your thrones like those of earthly kings,
Or low like milkmaids' stools?
Does your laughter sing like heavenly praise,
Your souls like shining jewels?
Does your love encompass everyone,
And treat all equally,
Or do you draw the Father's gaze

To behold your family?
Our hearts still stand before your tomb,
Your absence felt as pain,
Yet we cry out in faith and love,
We shall see you, sons, again!

Regretting lost opportunities with Matthew

Ah, my weary little boy,
Hold me close again,
Your arms wrapped tight around my neck
As I climb the stairs
To lay you in your bed,
To trace the cross upon your forehead,
To say, "I love you"
Before you drift to sleep.....

Your bed is gone now, Matthew,
Your clothes and bicycle, too,
But, most of all, your smile,
Your laugh,
The way you giggled
When I held your ticklish feet.

Oh, ask me to play with you again!
I'll leave the dishes, the laundry,
Forget the tiredness,
The reasons,
Excuses;

Oh, to see you smile at me,
To feel your love...
Do I really have to wait
Until I get to heaven, too?

$\mathcal{T}$omorrow he would have been

I saw him crown, kick, cry,
His life lending identity to my own,
The stages of his growth
Gauging the effectiveness of my fatherhood.
I wore with pride
The compliments of strangers,
And wondered what great deeds
My eldest son would one day achieve,
Never thinking it would be his death
Left to affect us all.
Tomorrow he would have been ten,
But he died just six months ago;
I still wake, and work... and grieve,
Thinking of him always.
He was of what was best in me,
And staring at his sleeping form
Caused vows to arise in me
To better myself for him,
To deserve him
And his love;
And so I shall continue to do.
I will always be proud
To be Andrew's dad.

Reaching out

Close your eyes, Maria,
For the world cannot bear your pain.
My heart hears your heart scream
For those two sons of ours who died.
Oh, how can we be living
When each breath moans,
Longing to hold them here again?
And now your mother-heart, half-beating,
Struggles to carry on.
There are walls around you now;
Your fragile heart can bear no more.
We find life in these other two -
Their living soothes our tears.

*O*n a sailing excursion with Karl -

Another mother learns of the accident

Dear gentle lady,
Thank-you for the tears
Your mother-heart shared
When you looked into her eyes.

Draw your son a little closer,
Feel his warmth against your side,
Caress his sandy wind-blown hair,
The fading chubbiness of his cheeks,
The poetry of his expressive mouth.

Do you see him now?

Of course,
For you live to gaze into his eyes;
That is why you cry:

She will never hold her little boys again.

Comfort from my angel

Gossamer white against the sun
My angel's wings enfolded me,
His eyes like swirling galaxies
Magnificent in their power,
The slightest movement of his thought
Mightier than a birthing sun.
"Ah, child," he whispered,
And distant mountains trembled,
"Your sons are now your brothers in the Lord."
And gazing heavenward with light-filled eyes, he said,
"Indeed, they are father-like,
For they shall parent you with their prayers."
He looked at me and knew I understood.
"How blessed are you to have such as these!" he cried,
The stars multiplying in his eyes,
The very glory of him bursting in the reflection of the Father's
Presence.
In that instant of complete joy,
His image vanished,
Though he remained,
And my tears of grief were changed to gratitude
And longing for the Lord.

ʄaith/emotion

Forgive these tears and burning heart
My son, my heaven-song,
For though my faith is telling me
You live in heaven now,
This pain remains and suffers me
To long for you now gone.
I laughed with you and carried you
Just hours before you died....

Eight months have passed
(Though days drag by)
Without your laugh, your smile.
My Matthew,
Hear your father's cry:
I love you, son!

Each new day reminds me
How blessed I was to have you those six years.
How those years have changed my life!

You're gone...

Yet here...

Though I can't see you -

This tortures me.

$\mathcal{A}$djusting my thinking

Some day my adult notions shall pass
About life and death and faith and doubt;
Some day I'll see the hand of God
In pain and joy and the tests of life;
Some day when I look back on all that was;
Some day when I stand with my sons who've gone before;
Some day when I see the face of God;
By the grace of God
I'll be a child of God,
Some day.

*H*earing a favorite song of AJ and Matthew

for the first time since the accident and after a fight with Maria

I heard you in the music played
In the timing and the tune;
In the meaning of the moment
When I needed to think of you.
"Try a little harder," you said,
"Give a little more than is 'right'."

Your faces impressed upon my mind
Do more to turn my will to love -
That I might be with you both again -
Than I on my own could ever do.

/t still doesn't seem real

How can you be gone?
You were always there,
Even before your conception -
We longed for you that much!
How many times I watched you sleep,
Wanting to be the father you deserved,
Planning the things we would do together,
The day we would speak man-to-man;
How can you be gone?
You helped me to be better -
Such was the power of loving you!
Let there be more than just these memories,
More than this bursting heart crying out:
From your place in heaven,
Help me still!

An allegory

Sigh to the sea
With agonies and sweet memories
Into her open arms;
Your journey now must end,
O little river,
Though she will receive you,
Carrying you to the ends of the world
Within her heaving heart
Where more shall be yours
Than could ever have been
Confined between your narrow shores.

Sunday at the crypt

I sat before their crypted portraits
And their crypted flowers,
And their crypted names in brass
On the crypted marble
In the crypted mausoleum,
And my crypted heart
Remembered the crypted Lord
WHO ROSE AGAIN
That nothing should be crypted anymore.

So I sat before their portraits
And their flowers,
And their names in brass
On the marble
In the mausoleum,
And my heart
Remembered the Lord
WHO ROSE AGAIN,
And my heart also rose
Thinking of my sons in heaven.

After just a glance at their portraits

The shadow of your absence
Lay across my searching heart,
For in picking up your portraits
I longed to see through your eyes again,
To have your perceptions affect my own
By the enjoyment of your being...alive.
My fingertips with their phantom memories
Slid slowly across the cold clear glass,
So much like the barrier that separates us,
Invisible, but without doubt...real.
Flashbacks of your actions,
Laughing, crying, sleeping faces
Filled and crushed my heart in milliseconds;
I cried out, sinking,
For the hand of Jesus
Walking with me on the sea of faith.

The testing

Its saccharine promise slithers in
In an unguarded moment;
Further into consciousness
Until the body can almost feel it,
And it seems to feel so... good.
Stand on guard, O intellect!
See with the eyes of faith!
Behind that sensuous tingle,
That burning thirst,
That gluttonous morsel,
That prideful glance,
That unfettered word,
That personal sin known to you and God,
Lies death of the soul.
Behind the enticing mask
Rots the devil's face,
And Satan wants your soul.

Whisper the name of Jesus
As though it were the last time,
As though you were out of time,
And all that was left
Was the Final Judgment;
Wouldn't you shout for mercy?

The good man sins seven times daily -
How many more those of us who are not!

How such thoughts dispel the fog of temptation,
And guide us on the way to heaven!

*finally able to write about November 29, 2008

I had four sons
Until that awful day of blood and agony.
The call no father wants to hear,
No mother wants to make,
Happened on that day
Of gasping, broken-hearted prayers:
O God!
O GOD!
PLEASE, NOT MY BOYS!
Yet, what if...?
Give me strength!
I clutched the steering wheel prie-dieu
With tear-choked Hail Mary-Hail Mary-Hail Marys,
Almost knowing what was to come
With numbed resignation.
Shaking hands fumbled coins at the meter apologetically -
My family was in a car accident.
The statement brings tears to my eyes.
Take your time, the strangers said,
Offering patience like a cool sweet drink.
- Into the place of brokenness and battered hope...
Surrounded, bandaged, intubated, unresponsive,
Side by side...
My sons.
I see the hesitant eyes of doctors and nurses,
(Will he break down?)
And the truth is there:
I shall never hear these sons speak,
Shall never look into their eyes,
Shall never laugh with them again.
I lean over each injured little boy,
Afraid to hurt them even more,
Wanting to get to them through soaked bandages and intrusive
tubes;
In my heart, they're in my arms.

I'm here...it's Daddy.
Whispered goodbyes sobbed softly;
Touching their faces one last time,
Again and again;
Their hair one last time,
Again and again;
Their arms, their hands, their fingers
Pressed to my lips;
It can never be enough.
My eyes bleed hot tears;
A low, aching moan
Escapes from two holes in my heart.
The last thing I can do for them:
Call the priest.
(Why doesn't he break down?)
Jesus holds me up.

O my wife's eyes!
Fearful, guilt-ridden, sorrowful mother -
Weeping and lamentation -
For two of her sons are no more!

Not you, too, Karl!
Please open your eyes;
Stay with us
With your poor broken body -
We need you, Son!
Lorenzo needs his big brother.
Ah, Lorenzo!
(Don't hug him so tightly!)
Look!
Flickering eyes!
Cries of joy while my torn heart
Wails for AJ and Matthew
Lying in cold silence,
Their candle-lit beds curtained off from the living.

I should have said I love you,
Not: Do up your seat belts.
Is it too late to say it now?

All in God's Time, My Sons

I love you, AJ!
I love you, Matthew!
I'm sorry I wasn't there to protect you.
(What could I have done?)
I love you, Sons,
Will always love you,
Relive in my heart
The times you said I love you to me...
Once in a while I may cry,
Because I miss you.
In heaven, you are like blossomed flowers;
I am still a seed.
In heaven, you speak the language of love;
I stutter in self-love.
In heaven, you are with God;
I still resist His grace.
Yet, your being there gives me peace,
Thanks be to God.

I had four sons
(And have them still -
Two rest in the Lord).

*f*riday meditation

Splayed across her lap,
The Lord lay, torn open,
His love exposed to the world.
She adored Him there
In the furnace of her raging heart
Pierced by the sword of Simeon.
It had all led to this:
The spotless Lamb sacrificed
To gain spotless grace for His mother,
That He might come
To make spotless the race
Condemned by Adam's fall,
Repeated in every soul since,
Save in only these two;
Yet, how He suffered for US!
And she for love of Him and us, her children!
How can she say thanks be to God
With His lifeless body in her arms?
With the blood and grime of His death
Matted against her cheek,
Pressed against her lips?
Her Son died for us.
Shouldn't she curse us?
If someone were responsible for the loss of your child's life,
Wouldn't you curse him?
Wouldn't I?
Yes.
And worse,
If not for the grace of God
And the prayers of His Mother,
Our Mother,
Who says thanks be to God
For now all her children
May go to heaven.
But, what of my sons' deaths?

Shall I say thanks be to God?
Shall I thank Him for their loss...
The loss of experiencing their growth
From childhood to manhood,
The loss of them physically present?
It is a loss keenly felt;
But mine, not the boys';
They are eternally happy;
What father wouldn't want that for his sons?
Shall I thank God
That AJ and Matthew were spared from pain
(Even in death),
And spared the possibility of turning away from God?
Yes, I thank You, Lord.
You know what is best.
I love You for taking my sons to Yourself
Where no evil may ever reach them
Safe in Your love.
I thank You that their deaths
Are a constant reminder
That no man knows the span of his own life,
And I keep watch, Lord.

*T*hey're not...here

I thought you would be here for the rest of my life,
To pray for me when I died,
Your wives and children beside you
(Or, possibly, you both concelebrating the funeral Mass).
To think I took your lives for granted,
Assumed there would be time
To do more,
To do better,
To plan for the future,
When I simply should have been grateful
Every day
That you were here.
That you...were.

$\mathcal{A}$ tender moment

Lift your lips to me
With their open promise,
And I into their gentle reception
Shall not betray your trust.
I enfold you in my arms
Where you are safe enough to cry,
For where in all the world
Could anyone understand
The loss of one's children
Except in the heart
Of the children's other parent?
Place your half-beating heart
Next to mine;
Together we shall bear this pain
Beating as one.

*I*ncentive

Sons,
You are...there,
With God;
Yet, God is here,
Everywhere.
Would it not be true, then,
To say
You are here, too?
Would it also be true to ask
Where you are not?
Souls are spirit.
How could the universe contain you?
There is no geography in heaven.
A soul is as great as its love;
For God is love.
Sin is the lack of love.
Sin is where you are not -
How I hate sin.

*G*ratitude

I saw the Lord today
In the dove-shaped cloud
Shining over the mausoleum;
I saw Him in the comfort given
As I wept before the crypt of my sons -
Tears of sorrow for the cross carried daily,
Tears of joy for the promised resurrection.
I saw the Lord today
In the welcoming arms of my wife,
In my sons: Karl pushing his wheelchair,
Lorenzo giggling at play;
In the family around me,
In the friends far and near,
The kindness of strangers,
The health of my body,
The roof over my head,
The food on my table,
The clothes on my back,
The work of my hands.
I saw the Lord today
In the faith that sustains me,
In the gifts from His love.

$\mathcal{A}$ visit

Do I have to move in sunlight
To feel its heat,
To see by its light?
Then hush, my soul;
Neither do I have to move
By thought
Or word,
Before the Blessed Sacrament
To be blessed by the heat of His love,
To be blessed by the light of His grace.

Gifts

My sons,
You walk the world
In eight human bodies -
Parts of you giving them life.
No, I don't want horrible images
Of who got what from where;
Let me imagine the smiling faces
Of these eight new children of mine
Sharing with their loved ones the fruit of life
Lovingly taken from the good earth of your deaths.
Such a bittersweet blessing!
How could they not weep joyfully
For their increased vitality,
Deeper breaths,
Stronger heartbeats,
The peace and joy of knowing
That when they kiss goodnight
They can kiss good morning, too?
Always in the back of their minds, though,
They know...
Someone's death gave them life;
Perhaps they know, too, that
That someone...
Was one of you, my sons.
You should be remembered,
Honored through their generations;
But, even should you be forgotten by them,
(Impossible!)
You are treasured by us,
Here,
And glorified in heaven,
My irreplaceable ones.

Visiting Westminster Abbey September 17, 2009

What caused the quickening in my heart
As I neared the abbey gate?
What caused the rising sorrow
At the steps of the church?
O, home of my soul!
I stumbled across your threshold
Bearing the palpable pain of the loss of my sons
For what might have been
Had they grown to manhood in my sight;
Perhaps then these oh so familiar bricks and pathways,
Liturgies and black-robed figures
Could have been experienced by AJ and Matthew as well
In days of seminary training -
AJ had intimated as much -
Instead, this peaceful haven
Remains a hospice for my battered soul,
And the cadence of Gregorian Chant
The balm for my anguished heart.
In time, my other sons may come visiting with me:
Karl, in his wheelchair,
Rolling silently through my recounted memories,
And Lorenzo,
Who could yet be called to this life,
Only God knows.
Meanwhile,
These sons who've gone before
Strengthen the monks
In the decades of their vowed observance;
AJ was named after St. Andrew,
My patron in monastic life,
And after St. Joseph,
The patron of the monastery;
And he was baptized on the feast of St. Benedict;
Matthew's middle name is Benedict,
After the great founder himself.

$\mathcal{V}$isiting the Poor Clares in Mission

Ah, Sisters,
Though you build your home
On the highest mountain,
In the hottest desert,
In the remotest forest
Seeking the Lord in solitude,
Yet shall we come
In all our suffering aspects
To meet the Lord in you.
We long to see His compassion
In your eyes,
To feel His love
In your smiles,
To lay our burdens
At your feet;
For you have the ear of God
When you raise your voices in prayer,
And you lift us to His heart
With the insistent love of mothers.

*d*are I say it

It is said of Adam's sin:
"O, Happy Fall",
Because, through his sin,
The Savior came to redeem us.
Dare I say,
O, blessed accident?
Two sons are in heaven,
Safe from all evil,
And the unceasing thought of them
Draws me closer to God
As the ultimate incentive
To achieve the Beatific Vision they enjoy.

*I*n communion

The Lord sat enthroned within my heart,
His temple,
Among the temples gathered
On the Day of the Lord.
It pleased Him
That I worshiped His presence,
And He smiled from His throne;
He had something to give me!
Suddenly they shone beside Him,
Exulting to be near Him!
Jesus laughed at the joyous laughter of my sons,
Their jumping more like dancing.
AJ beamed, endlessly smiling.
(Yes, I see you, AJ,
Just let me look at you)
Matthew smiled, and smiled, and smiled.
(Ah, Mateo, Mateo,
You are glowing with so much... LIFE!)
My boys!
How I love you!
I am so happy you are with the Lord!
It thrilled them knowing I understood:
To spend time with them,
I had to spend time with the Lord.
When I receive the Lord in Communion,
I receive heaven as well;
Then my sons can come to me
As long as His presence remains.
Together we can worship,
They in the Beatific Vision,
I in the faith prayed for each day.
Too soon His presence left me,
Though leaving me with a greater desire for Communion,
And unending union,
Some day.

The grace of motherhood

She sat weeping hours before the dawn
With joyful images of our departed sons
Playing on the computer screen before her,
Her eyes like arms reaching out to them,
Her heart unable to contain the ocean of longing
Overflowing from eyes as wide as the gulf between life and death,
Her sobs unanswered moans from a pleading heart.

I held her there,
The struggling storm within the circle of my love,
And I loved her more for the depth of her love
Refusing to feel anything less
Simply because two sons were not present in her arms –
They were forever in her heart –

O the strength of woman!

At the sweet sound of: "Mom!" from our waking sons,
She hid the furious tempest within her
And rose in the grace of motherhood
Answering the call of love,
And poured out double upon them –
All she had to give.

*H*ow did I do it then

I folded your clothes
After you died
And gave them all away,
Keeping for myself the cap
Embroidered with your name.
I hid it in a box
Like those memories of you
Sealed in my heart,
Locked behind walls
Where I walk sometimes
And no one can see me cry.

*f*or our good

Be assured of this:
To achieve your salvation
God may smash all you hold dear,
If need be.
God sacrificed His only Son for us.
Do you think
He would think twice
About crushing your comforts,
Permitting illness to ravage you,
Or taking your loved ones to be with Him,
If it would turn your attention to eternity -
To Him?
He loves you enough
To risk your anger,
Even hatred,
For hate is closer to love
Than complacency,
Indifference,
Apathy,
Lukewarmness.
How could suffering in this life -
30, 60, 100 years? -
Compare with eternity?
If such suffering led to union with the Lord,
Would it not be seen as blessing
And a gift of God's love
In the light of eternity?

St. Matthew's Day, September 21

On St. Matthew's day,
I wondered about little St. Matthew,
My son,
Just six-years-old when he went to heaven.
Do all the Matthews in heaven
Celebrate the great apostle's day
In honor of the first saint to bear their name?
How would my little Matthew fare
In an ocean of older Matthews
Gathered before the Lord?
I imagined the holy men parting like the Red Sea,
But, rather than with Moses' staff,
Love and humility made way for my son;
As their hearts were open,
So the gathered Matthews opened,
And gently urged him forward
Until he stood before the Lord
Rejoicing in the love and humility in their souls.
My Matthew smiled in the arms of the Savior,
A smile that glorified God
And filled the gathered Matthews with joy.

$\mathcal{B}$aptism Day, September 26

I awoke in joy
On my Baptism Day:
My wife sleeping beside me,
Lorenzo snuggled between,
Karl calling good morning
From his bed in his room.
Alleluia! Cried my soul,
Prompted by the Lord,
For his grace resounds within me,
Baptized by Fr. Joseph Adam O.M.I.
(May he be blessed in heaven)
In Our Lady of Victory Parish
Forty-four years ago today.
Alleluia!
I am a child of God!
Alleluia! Cried my soul
At the rising of the sun,
Like Jesus,
Into open-armed blue skies,
Like Our Lady's mantle over all.
Alleluia!
Let's go to Jesus
Through the heart of the Blessed Virgin Mary.
Alleluia!
AJ and Matthew in heaven,
Sing praises to the Father
For your father
On his Baptism Day.

San Lorenzo Day, September 28

San Lorenzo,
The needs of your people call to you
For they suffer greatly today
From storms and floods,
Hunger and poverty.
Forgive them if the struggle to survive
Causes them to forget you;
It is hard to pray
On an empty stomach,
Cradling a dying child,
Weeping over the corpse of someone who drowned.
Hear my prayer
From one in a comfortable country
Where comfort flows
Like clean water from a faucet,
Where it is easy to pray...
When we feel like it.
My son is named for you,
Which makes me believe you'll hear
And lift the needs of your homeland
To our Father with your prayers
On this, your feast day,
San Lorenzo Ruiz, we pray!

first anniversary of becoming a Benedictine oblate

When our forefathers in faith,
The ancient Jews,
Worshiped in the temple,
Their sacrificial offerings
Were burned on the great stone altar.
Was it not enough
That they be offered
Rather than be burned to ashes?
Perhaps the answer lay in that
The sacrifice belonged wholly to God,
Making it holy,
And any other use would lessen it,
Profane it;
No higher purpose could be given,
Not even feeding the poor.

We Christians are also sacrificial offerings to God,
To be consumed in His love,
To be holy
For His purposes,
To make up what is lacking in the sufferings of Christ.
How could it be enough
To merely offer our obedience
But not obey?
To carry the cross of Christ
But feel no pain?
Who else could the Lord ask to suffer
For those who do not yet know Him
If not members of His own Body?

And this is also what being an oblate means:
Living as a sacrificial offering to God,
Allowing the Lord to consume us in the fire He chooses,
For His divine plan.
When I kneel before the altar at Mass

In the moments before the bloodless Sacrifice,
Before Jesus offers Himself as a sacrifice to the Father,
And to us as spiritual food,
I unite my lifelong offering to the death of Jesus:
My sons taken so early
And my heart bearing this cross
On the way to the Resurrection.

*T*en months

Have ten months been long enough
To never cry again?
No, nor would ten years;
That is what love does -
It never ends.
That they are dead
Makes me realize
I love them more than I was aware,
Makes me realize
How much I need to love
My sons who yet remain
And have them know it.
That casual "Bye, Dad,"
Could be the last I ever hear;
And when I say my own goodbyes,
"I love you," must be there
To embrace them on the way,
Wherever it may lead.
Ten months have been long enough
To let me cry
At heart pangs
Triggered by sights and sounds and reminiscences;
To let me laugh
At memories, yes,
And life's pleasures, too.
Ten months have been long enough
To teach me to live
And love
Today.

St. Michael the Archangel, September 29

O, mighty angel of the Lord,
I wondered why you chose to favor me
With unexpected images and reminders of you
Leading to the day I became an oblate of St. Benedict -
And I unaware it was your feast day!
Only afterward I remembered
I had prayed your chaplet (poorly) years before,
Being impressed with devotion for you
In the heart of a good priest.
Was that enough to earn your favor?
Or, could you see the trial to come,
Knowing I would need your powerful aid?
Or did the great St. Benedict pray for me,
And raise the gift of my oblation to the Father
Who granted me your faithful friendship
To bear me up through the deaths of my sons?
O, St. Michael the Archangel,
Beat back temptation too great for me to bear
With the protection of your flaming sword,
Or, lift me with wing-like inspiration from its subtle grasp.
Let angels from the heavenly ranks in your command
Surround my little family,
And hourly bear our messages of love
To my sons with you there.
Each morning I call upon you -
(In such a little way!)
Trusting you to be with me
Through whatever the day shall bring.

$\mathcal{T}$o the other driver

I learned your name today
In a letter from my son's lawyer;
It caught me off guard
To see it there in print,
Stated coldly:
Involved in 'proceedings' -
Why did it take ten months to learn this simple fact?
Simple?
What is this heaviness in my heart,
This shallow breathing,
This flood of questions:
Who are you?
What are you like?
What do you believe?
What was going through your mind
Before...and after...
Did you think about saying sorry?
Did you want to,
But choked on the inadequacy of words?
Did someone advise you not to?
Did seeing your own child that night -
Happy, healthy...home -
Almost tear you apart?
Has that tragic decision,
To pull into the wrong lane,
Replayed itself nightmarishly in your mind
Until, desperately, in self-defense,
Anger rose within you
At how your life was unalterably changed,
Convincing yourself to be the one wronged?
Or, were you advised so?
- I don't know, you haven't spoken to me -
I caught glimpses of my deceased sons' photographs
Just moments ago -
YOU are the reason I will never hold them again;

YOU.... I cannot be angry -
They would not want me to be
Because they are in heaven...
And... you never intended the harm you caused
(It would be too horrible to think otherwise!).
I must focus on my wife
And my surviving sons;
They need my attention and energy.
I wish you no harm -
Even if you believe yourself to have done nothing wrong -
That is between you and the courts...
You and God.

$\mathcal{D}$ear Guardian Angel

O, inseparable companion!
You show yourself
In such subtle ways:
Inspiring thought and suggestion,
Reproach, too, if need be!
Does my failing to listen anger you?
What happens between us
When I sin?
Is there a 'thickening' of the veil
Between flesh and soul,
An increase in the fog
Between me and God?
Or, could it be described as distance
Since, by sinning,
I run away from God?
This much is clear:
God reaches out , I pull back,
Blinding my intellect,
Hardening my heart,
Weakening my desire for God.
Do you get frustrated at my stupidity,
Or do you remember even angels,
With their superior intellects
And no concupiscence to contend with,
Fell, too?
In mortal sin,
Do I force you far from me?
And, at such times (Lord, deliver me!),
Do you fall prostrate before the Lord in prayer...
For me?
Do you 'walk' with me in everything -
Joys and sorrows,
According to the will of the Lord?
When I strive to live in grace,
Do you beam with joy,

56 --

The veil thinning,
The fog lifting,
The distance lessening?
Is the presence of the Lord
In the temple of my soul
The fulfillment of God's plan for you?
Or will that be satisfied
When we both bow before the Lord,
Worshipping Him together?
Let's make a pact, you and I:
Guide me on the way to heaven,
And I will strive to follow!

Creation speaks of the glory of God

The bright full moon
Shone eucharistic
In a monstrance of sculpted clouds,
And distant stars dimly sparkled,
As saints and angels do,
In humble adoration.

Day and night creation sings,
Reflects, and speaks of truths
Spiritual and divine
To turn men's thoughts
To prayer and praise
For the Artisan of Life.

Jesus humbly hides Himself
Under the form of bread
In the flickering glow of candles,
Waiting for the light of faith
To rise in the heart of one
Believing enough to visit Him.

The Author and Finisher of our faith
Watches over us through the long night
And into the light of day,
The glorious sun a pale reflection of His glory.
He gives life, and is Life,
The Truth, the Way.

I could never have known

Every day I prayed,
"Watch over my boys, Lord,
Keep them healthy...
And safe...
And, above all, close to You."
After the accident someone said to me,
"It must be your worst nightmare
To have two sons die
On the same day."
No.
Far worse would have been
Having them die as young men,
And not know the state of their souls -
Whether they were far from You,
Or safe with You.
AJ and Matthew were so young!
This gives me confidence and peace,
For You said, "Let the little children come to Me,"
And Your Holy Church reaffirmed this in her prayers
On the day we laid my sons to rest.
My sons...
Your souls, because You died for them,
Purchased them with Your blood.
You gave them to me, Lord,
Receive them
Baptized into Your Death and Resurrection.
You answered my prayer
To keep them close to You,
Although I could never have known this would be the way.
It is better they go to You as children
Than die far from You as men.

To carry them with us

Forgive me if my thoughts seem elsewhere,
Intent on subjects other than yours.
It's true;
I linger longingly on their memory,
The better not to forget
The inflection of their laugh
Like music I only now fully appreciate,
And the smallest mannerisms,
Like memorable details defining the whole.
They were here,
Once,
Affecting every aspect of my world;
Now that they have gone,
Should the unpreventable act of living
Wash over the memory of them
Like waves over castles in the sand?
They did live;
They were here
And no one could ever fill the holes
Left by their absence.
Our family circle draws closer
Finding comfort in we who remain,
In speaking of sons and brothers -
The relationships we bound ourselves with love -
In sharing reminiscences,
Weaving them into the fabric of our present
To carry them with us,
For they are alive
In the unforgettable, undeniable effect
Their lives express upon our own;
And then we smile...
It is then when the pain can co-exist with joy
We are able to lift our eyes, our hearts, our souls
To consider the life we are meant to live
If we would be truly alive -
As they.

Paradox

I notice warmth upon my face -
How good it feels;
Something so simple, so basic in life,
Being able to enjoy sunshine, blue sky,
Clouds in all their shapes and sizes,
A refreshing breeze...
I smile,
And it stabs me to the heart
Finding joy when two of my sons
Are not here to share it,
As though it is wrong to be happy
Since they died just ten months ago;
As though all joy must be connected to them.
Life goes on, they say,
And I suppose it does -
Breathe in... and out... in... and out,
And another day goes by -
If you choose to live that way.
I think it better to accept the sorrow that comes with loss,
Making life that much sweeter;
Perhaps the warmth of sunshine
Meant less ten months ago,
And the possibility of this being my last day
Helps me enjoy the littlest things
And truly appreciate the most important -
My wife and my other sons -
Ironically, it is this submission to what cannot be changed
That lifts us into freedom to enjoy what can.

The goodness of others

They reached out to us
And moved us to tears
With the latent goodness dwelling in people
Needing but the right motivation
To release a tidal wave of caring.
By showering us with loving concern,
They assuaged their own pain caused
By the pain we went through,
Intensified when looking into their children's eyes
And praying, "Please... never my children..."
Or meeting the eyes of spouses
Refusing to speak the possibility,
For thinking it was pain enough.
They reached out, lifted, and carried us,
And we appreciated each loving act.

Well-known people, organizations and corporations
Drew us in, supported us,
Used connections and influence
To bring smiles to the face of a paralyzed boy,
And were amazed at our son's attitude and resilience,
Possibly wondering if they could handle paralysis
And the loss of two brothers
As well as this nine-year-old boy.
The generosity with their time,
The giving of themselves,
Brought joy to my wife and me
By seeing our son laugh,
Reinforcing our desire that Karl
Live beyond his disability.

Thank-you seems inadequate
When said so many times.

The rosary

My wilted roses strewn at Our Lady's feet
Are picked up, lovingly
Arranged in beautiful bouquets
Given to the Lord
By the Blessed Virgin herself;
My inattentive prayers,
Clothed in her blue mantle,
Receive His undivided attention.
That pressing concern,
That impossible situation,
That unbearable problem
Seemingly corrects itself
With my only involvement being
Trust in Mary's prayer.

The beauty of this unreclaimable loss

Sometimes I pause in the course of my actions
To consciously place your faces before my mind
Overwhelmed by how much I miss you.
Compelled, I fling back the door across my heart,
Reaching out to the memory of you;
The pain of these remembrances
Crushes my chest,
And, open-mouthed, I gasp to breathe,
Blinking away the surging tide of tears,
Pushed back even now,
After these many months;
Even now,
When no one can see.
I hold the memories of my life with you
Like diamonds, to the light;
The many-faceted interactions flash and shine.
In my mind,
I weep for the beauty of this unreclaimable loss
While, in reality,
I pour out the blood and tears of my heart
Through the catharsis of my pen,
Enlisting an army of mourners on my behalf.

Days of remembrance

The spent and golden leaves like scattered graces fall,
Reminders of this fleeting life;
And, bundled against the autumn chill,
I approach the days of remembrance
Praying for the grace to bear them;
For the days of November toll mournfully,
Loudly and with solemn tones
until the 29th day
When the desire for spoken words is hushed
Lest, in opening my mouth,
I betray the illusion of my own strength.
Mourning shall cloak this day always -
However long always shall be for me -
For only God knows the length of one's life.
If my sons' sudden deaths taught anything,
It is that there is no future,
Only now;
Only now to live and love.
Bittersweet are life's joys
Often ending too soon, or poorly;
Bittersweet life's sadnesses
Sometimes tempered with blessings.
Bitter... sweet -
To keep my mind on the beauty of God
Alone unfading and unchanging.

$\mathcal{T}$o be alive

It is good to be alive,
To worship the Lord and serve Him;
To make my wife, sons, relatives and friends smile;
To receive love and give love;
It is good to be alive,
To see the faces of loved ones, rainbows, stars and children;
To hear music, wind, voices, singing and laughter;
To touch warm skin, the bark of trees, snow balls and puppy fur;
To taste ice cream, sour candies, barbecued chicken and beer;
To smell clean babies, flowers, food cooking and fallen leaves;
It is good to be alive,
To strive, achieve, marvel, wonder, praise, glorify;
It is good to be alive...
To be.

*I*magination

When I 'see' my angel comforting me,
Or 'see' my deceased sons at my side during Mass,
Or 'see' the Lord smiling from the consecrated Host,
Some may say it is just my imagination.
Perhaps.
Nevertheless, I thank the Lord
For this wonderful creation
Giving invention, poetry, art and writing,
Reflections of God's creative power,
This blessing through which inspiration may flow
As in the dreams of St. Joseph,
Or earlier in the dreams of the patriarch Joseph in Egypt,
Giving peace and comfort,
Leading closer to God -
Signs of the Holy Spirit at work.

Your bodies held captive

What is this need drawing me
To sit before your tomb?
I sit as closely as I can to your bodies
Once cradled, wrestled, held and carried,
Your bodies held captive
Behind this marble-walled death
Destroying these temples of God,
And reducing them to dust and ash,
The punishment for Adam's sin
When the devil thought he had won;
But, you shall rise again
As did the Lord,
Though your third day be perhaps three thousand years from
now;
You shall rise gloriously
Filled with the presence of God for eternity,
Higher than the angels as Sons of God,
Heaping coals upon that fallen angel's malice.
All in good time;
All in God's time, my sons;
We shall be together again.
For now, I pull myself away
Leaving your precious bodies
In the care of others
Never loving you as I.

The beating Host

Prompted by the Lord,
I adored Him in His chapel
In the parish named for His Body.
Bowing low, I threw roses at His feet
With the beads of Our Lady slipping through my fingers.
I raised my eyes to behold the Host
Enthroned in His humble monstrance
And blinked to clear my sight,
For the Host throbbed!
The edges became irregular
And the Host seemed thick
Like flesh.
The beating seemed the beating of a heart,
And faint lines crossed the Host
Giving the impression
I beheld the very muscle of the Sacred Heart!
I looked away again and again,
Yet still the beating Host remained.
O Lord! I cried,
Never shall I look at You in the Blessed Sacrament
The same way again!
Take this image from me
If not from You,
And, if from You,
Cause such a miracle
As to draw all to Your Presence!
At times, the Host became transparent
As though the Lord were showing me
The accidental was a mirage
While the substance was the truth;
The bread was not present,
HE was!
How does one withdraw from the LORD GOD making Himself
known?
By desiring to live better for Him,

To enthrone His Presence within.
Perhaps faith lived through love
Strengthens the sight of the soul;
This passing world is an accidental
And life with God the substance.

*L*iving memories

I catch myself staring at my surviving sons
For the sheer joy of being able to see them;
I stroke the hair on their heads
And cannot help thinking of their brothers,
That the last time I touched them
Their bodies lay cold before the altar.
I wanted my fingers to memorize those sensations then,
So that, when closing my eyes,
I could feel their hair, their skin
By reaching out to their memory
With my hand raised before me,
But find instead living memories of Matthew
In the tilt of Lorenzo's head,
And the thick dark hair of AJ
While resting my hand on Karl's head.
At times, I resist the urge
To clutch Lorenzo and Karl too tightly,
And shudder at the thought of losing them, too.
I push the thought from me
And turn to savour the sublime moment
Of cuddling, hugging, playing, laughing with my sons
As though nothing else mattered.

They would share what I feel

There are times
When I would like to stop strangers on the street;
"Let me tell you about my boys,"
I would say;
And, with no prior knowledge
Or preconceived ideas
About me or my sons,
They would share what I feel,
Would become, like me,
Waves crashing on the rocks
Of immovable mourning,
Forming an ocean, sighing,
Sometimes sobbing,
For the loss of these boys
And others taken tragically.
Storms of emotion surge sometimes,
Then abate upon a glassy calm...
Sorrow flows more gently
Borne in the heart of human compassion
And the loving support of others.

The way things have come to be

I miss AJ greeting me
When I would come home;
And when, visiting me at work in the park,
He would run across the field to meet me.
I remember it sometimes,
Turning the doorknob at home,
Passing the grassy picnic areas in the park...
I can still see AJ smiling,
His arm waving
As though I would not have known it was him
From far away.
Oh, the days when,
Just last year,
I was surrounded proudly by my four sons!
I would wake in the morning
With them piling on my bed;
And, shrieking wide-eyed gleefully,
They would run from me getting up
And growling like a bear.
Matthew called it playing monster;
For Lorenzo, I am a dinosaur.
Yes, Lorenzo,
I will give you a horsey-back ride,
And re-live the memories
Of your brothers doing the same,
And hide my sorrow for your not remembering
AJ and Matthew playing with you.
Ah, my Karlito,
How do I connect with you
Through the wheelchair freeing you,
Yet restricting you, too?
I must come to your bed now
To greet you in the morning,
And tickle you above the level of your paralysis.
My grief for your loss of mobility and sensation

Must lie still in my heart,
Unmoving as your legs,
For you bravely bear this
And the absence of AJ and Matthew
While I could walk away in search of distraction
(As though that were possible)
From the way things used to be,
And from the way things have come to be
With the weight of irreversible change.

AJ, intercessor

Watch Karl's face light up telling jokes,
How he leans back in his wheelchair,
His mouth opened wide with glee,
His hands and arms expressive,
His feet and legs motionless -
He reaches out from his confinement
To draw you into his world -
Do not feel guilty about enjoying the life of this surviving son
Because two others have died;
I see the guarded thoughts,
The stifled emotions
Hidden in your heart...

I love you, too, Daddy.

I see the number of your days
In the mind of God -
Only a little while longer, Daddy -
What is earthly life
When compared to eternity?
I will give each tear to Jesus -
"Look how much my Daddy loves me," I'll say -
And offer it for you, and Mommy, and Karl, and Lorenzo
If you offer each tear, too,
And remember me at Mass.

Matthew said he loves you, too,
And to tell Mommy
He loves her more than the happiness of heaven...
He would trade places with her
Just to make her smile.
There are no goodbyes
When I am closer than the air...

God bless, God bless, God bless.

Send an angel of inspiration

Let fall your inspiration, Lord,
And guide my thoughts to pen
Such words as move the heart
To tears and prayer made resolute
In steadfast faith and love.
Send an angel of inspiration
Whose whispered counsels
Settle imperceptibly, though
With profound consequence
And obvious illumination,
Providing guidance undeniably
Heaven-sent.

November 29, 2009

I stand, shaking, upon the threshold
Of this terrible day of remembrance,
This anniversary of the death of my sons,
Of emotions and firsts that shall never come again:
The first Christmas without AJ and Matthew,
The first springtime,
The first birthday -
Their birthdays forever marked with 'would have been' -
This day could have been a precipice
From which hopes and dreams would perish
Dashed upon rocks of depression and disbelief;
This day, rather, shall be a vantage point,
Preparatory,
To gaze with faith and love
Into the infinite beauty of life with God,
Which, indeed,
We are able to begin here and now.

I choose Faith, and Hope, and Love,
My mind focused on my smiling sons
Beckoning with prayers and encouragement
Just out of sight,
Across the finish line,
Where they wait,
Unable to express the beauty of God.

Time

Time has nothing left for my son AJ;
Yet, how strange it seems my firstborn son
Shall be remembered forever as nine-years-old,
Though agelessly wise in God's presence,
While December 14th marks the date
Karl shall surpass his earthly age.
How shall Karl look back years from now
Remembering AJ and Matthew
As he matures into manhood and old age?
For he was merely eight-years-old -
And time moves faster as one grows -
For me, it shall seem like yesterday,
Though I live to be ninety-five,
When I waved and watched them drive away
Never to see them alive again.
Oh, stern taskmaster, Time,
You cannot fool me
With your exacting visage,
Exempting none from your predetermined tallies!
Smile, my friend,
For each day marked on your timesheet
Brings me closer to my boys!

*I*n the moments between

I parted the curtains
Enclosing the bodies of my sons
And staggered back at the finality of their deaths;
Those cold shells, those empty husks
Were not my boys!
Yet, I longed to hold them
Before the locked clasps of their coffins
Sealed those former temples of the Spirit
From my arms, my eyes,
Leaving me to seek comfort in photographs
When even the camera strained to capture them;
They were filled with so much life!
I remember that moment of realization now,
As the first year without them ends.
I searched for blessings in their deaths -
Those who received life-saving organs,
The strengthening of community -
And seek deeper meaning in the Spirit;
As no gift is given (or suffering permitted)
Solely for an individual's benefit (or testing),
But for those around him as well,
Like faith (or doubt), wisdom (or lack of judgment), wealth (or
poverty),
So the deaths of my sons speak to me
In their dying in moments between the week ending
And the Lord's Day dawning;
In moments between the Church year ending
And another beginning;
In the inevitable process of decay,
Death sudden or distant,
And the hope of resurrection and glory!
The deaths of Andrew and Matthew
Bridge old and new, death and life,
Shouting: Be prepared!
And, Come, Lord Jesus!

I long for faith's fulfillment,
The consummation of all things in God,
And reunion with my sons in the Vision of God.

*M*atthew speaks of heaven

I did not feel the blow of death -
No pain or sad decline -
One moment I sat among my family,
Then time ceased to exist for me;
I am in God's presence always.
Six years were as a dream,
As unreal in the sight of God
As the possibility of losing heaven!
I was baptized,
And I am home with God my Father...
Eternally!
That was me and AJ at the funeral, Dad;
In your soul you know it!
We asked Jesus to let you see us
Because we want to thank you for eternity!
And Jesus does approve of the faith you passed on
(You know that, too!),
Allowing us to enter heaven.
I never left your love,
But carry it always before the Lord.
Such a weak word, Daddy!
Love is so much more in the Heart of God!
Having no body,
When I say I love you,
My soul exists as love
And would be willing to cease existing
That you might know Love as I know Him.
When AJ told you
I love Mommy more than the happiness of heaven,
It's true!
I pray for her always,
Would take away her grief and guilt,
And all that troubles her,
If I could;
But, God permits me only to pray for her

And Karl and Lorenzo, too.
If Mommy could see how hard I pray for her
And love her before the Lord,
The times I snuggled with her
Would seem mere courtesies!
All is joy, Daddy!
I love you!
God is All! God is All! God is All!

*H*eavenly garments

What now, my soul?
What lies beyond the barrier of time
Tomorrow, next week, next month, next year?
How many years shall pass
Before the portraits of my youthful sons
While I age more and more?
Pointless to ask such things,
For there may not be a tomorrow for me,
Yet, still I wonder;
And, in wondering,
Resolve to keep my sons ever present
Lest the message of their deaths
Be blunted by the growing gap
Between their deaths and mine unknown.
I shall write of them,
Shall write to them,
And, with the needle of my pen,
Knit each precious moment
With their eternal now -
My thoughts, my prayers, my words,
With theirs -
Stitching the imperceptible space between
Into garments for eternity.

*U*rgency

...And in my dream,
A strange constellation seemed to appear
In the night sky overhead;
I watched as it drew nearer,
And discerned it to be a mirror image of the earth,
Transparent, except for the continents, which glowed;
And our continent positioned itself overhead,
Then country, province, city, neighbourhood,
And the very place where I stood also appeared.
Closer and closer it came,
The space between narrowing as though crushed.
Then shouts of alarm echoed everywhere.
A solemn voice from heaven spoke,
In words I cannot recall,
Though all standing near me, and I,
Thought the Coming of the Lord Jesus Christ was upon us.
I grasped my rosary
And wondered if there yet remained time for prayer,
Penance, and works of mercy.
The voice spoke,
And examples of people living in impoverished countries
Who yet sacrificed greatly for God
Were shown us in the image overhead,
And we were shamed in our comfortable homes.
And the vision meant us to reflect upon our lives,
Upon the feebleness of our giving
And our living for the Lord;
Everyone watching desired to seek out the poor and the needy,
To atone for failings in charity;
We hungered to love God
And repented the wasted attention given mere trifles;
But, held immobile,
We were forced to recognize our spiritual poverty.
We feared the Lord would come
Before we could amend our lives;

Such an agony came upon us
That we should be found wanting in the eyes of God
And had realized it too late!

The alarm clock woke me,
And I wondered at the power of my dream,
Leaving the impression of urgency;
Truly the Lord is coming!

for D.G.

Seeing the pearl of great price,
Holding it in your soul...
Ah, dear sister,
(Sister of my soul),
What need is there for words
When the Lord Himself walks in the garden of your soul
Planting seeds of faith and hope and love,
And tending virtues grafted from His Sacred Heart?
You glimpse with the eyes of faith,
Though dimly, as through a shimmering mist,
The promised life with God
Causing such an ache in your soul
That heaven should be so close,
And you knowing it to be unattainable;
Heaven is received,
Not acquired;
And, like the purest lover,
You must pine, and court, and prove
Patiently over the course of your God-given life
The worth of your love.
Though all the world turn from you,
He would not.
Would you from Him?
The answer in your heart
Begins your heaven now.
The fire of love grows
Through trials permitted you by the Lord,
And also by your messages of love to Him
Until you are aglow,
And would have all around you
Believe the same,
Love the same;
Yet, though the Lord set you, unknowing,
As a light of love to draw others to Him,
Not all shall love Him as you do,

Nor even know Him,
Nor even desire to know Him.
This painful side of love shall grow, too,
As the Lord draws you to Himself;
And, though you would draw those closest with you,
That is best left to the merciful Lord
With your confident cries of: Jesus, I trust in You!

*L*ittle gusts of wind

I stood on the fenced pavement
outside your little school
As memories of you both playing there
Swirled around me
Like little gusts of wind.
I used to stand... just there, waiting for you,
In the moments after classes ended.
You would smile, seeing me,
And let me hug you and take your bags
Before you would run off to play
As I waited for your brother, too.
How is it I almost heard your voices
Though I stood alone;
Were the echoes of your laughter still so strong
A year after you died?
I loved seeing your faces bright with excitement,
And the comforted look of recognition in your eyes.
The memories of those lost smiles
Spun like fallen leaves
On the barren pavement,
My sighs silenced in strong November winds.
I still have your brother,
Thanks be to God,
And how different 'school' is now
With his wheelchair, ramp and stairclimber!
Does he not miss what was?
Has he no complaints to make?
Is he not tempted to rail against the loss of the use of his legs
And the loss of you, his brothers?
I am so proud of him!
His acceptance strengthens me,
And shakes me out of melancholy.
Your faces shine so much brighter
When I remember you are in heaven,
When I allow the winds of memory
To be enveloped by winds of grace.

$\mathcal{T}$he emissary

Death approaches nearer with each breath.
I know it comes,
Though I know not when;
Nevertheless, I mean to greet it open-hearted,
This emissary of the Lord,
For it can do nothing
Unless permitted by my God;
And death's summons
Is the invitation to the banquet
Promised by the Lord.
It is a moment, a twinkling,
A 'putting an end to time',
The rending of the veil
Separating God's temple in my body
From the Holy-of-Holies in His Presence.
Shall death come gently,
As I sleep, perhaps,
And I waking to eternal joy?
(Not likely, since only saints go straight to Heaven.)
Or, shall death first bring pain
As through sickness or accident?
The final result would be the same,
Though, perhaps, pain would be necessary
To expiate all trace of sin
And be the means of one last sacrifice for the Lord.
Much to be preferred (the saints tell us) a painful death
Rather than expiation in Purgatory!
It seems to me the tolling bells of funerals
Should be followed soon by hopeful peals of joy,
For life is but a preparation for death,
That doorway into eternal Life!
It would be sad to leave my wife and sons,
Though it would be joyful to join my other sons in glory
Seeing my God as He is!

God's will be done.
Come, emissary,
And may your summons find me ready
On the day my time runs out!

forgotten and safe in heaven

The far horizon of what could be
May often be revealed in the scene at hand;
As the strength of the sun at midday
May be promised in the clear sky at dawn,
As the birth of a child
May be promised in the moment of conception;
So the promise of heaven
May be revealed in a soul turning to God.
Is the same to be said for the close of this year?
Might the promise of an end to separation be here?
To see my sons again!
It is easy to speak of an end following a beginning;
But what of all that shall come between?
And for how long?
To someone, someday, looking back,
It may not seem so long or so great a thing -
The summary of a life -
For even ages of the world
Can be reduced to paragraphs
Skimmed easily in history books.
Perhaps my great-great-grandchildren
(Should God grant them)
Might tell it in a line:
Two of his sons died when nine and six,
And he when such-and-such.
And to the world I might be no more
Than a genealogical anecdote,
An essential ancestor on a family tree.
The trials and deeds of my life
Might be remembered by God alone,
Which would be fine with me,
As long as I could be forgotten
And safe with my sons in heaven.

$\mathcal{A}$ favour for St. Andrew's Day

You had no feast day last year, St. Andrew,
Since November 30th fell on a Sunday,
And my car-killed sons awoke from death
On the Day of the Lord.
Did you present them to the Lord
Since my Andrew was named for you?
And did he immediately show concern for us
As he usually did... before?
And, reassured that God had seen our needs,
Did he hold my Matthew around the shoulder
And lead him to the Lord?
No doubt, no doubt...
That was AJ's way.
A year has passed.
Not for me do I ask this, St. Andrew,
I believe my sons are happy and with the Lord;
Give my wife a sign from heaven,
A sign of love from AJ and Matthew,
For she suffers from their loss
Through guilt, and sorrow
That only a mother's heart could feel.
I would not want to bear
The sights and sounds she bears from the accident;
And she may remember it all tomorrow
On its first terrible anniversary,
And on the Day of the Lord, too!
Such a heavy cross to bear in the light of the Resurrection!
Let Sunday pass in peace,
Then hear my prayer, dear patron of monastic days,
And may the Lord grant a special gift
To heal my wife with love,
And mark St. Andrew's Day with joy!

Refuge

Once again
The monastic calm enveloped me,
The lush grounds veiled in mist and rain.
I found You, as always, in the chapel,
Your tabernacle unmoved,
Your patient Presence present still,
Welcoming both priest and prodigal
As in every Catholic chapel around the world;
Though here the listening silence
Invites the contemplation of You
In quiet freed from clamouring cries
Of the self-important city
Where Your hidden Presence
Is too often forgotten
In the bustling busy-ness of life.
Yet the many troubles in the world
Find their succour here,
Shouldered by the prayers of monks both young and old,
Compelled to satisfy in charity
The longing of Your Heart
That all should find their refuge in You,
Their Savior and their Lord.

$\mathcal{T}$hose people

"I hope you've written something happy," you said,
Barely one year since the death of my sons;
You who could see your children every night,
If you wished;
You who could call your children on the telephone
If you missed the sound of their voices;
You who could invite your children to dinner
To drink in the sight of them.
Even should a day go by without their presence,
You know your children are alive...
"Something happy," you said.
Perhaps the anniversary of the funeral
In just one week
Must pass first;
Perhaps, too, the grey days of winter.
What exactly do you mean by 'happy'?
I am 'happy' my sons are in heaven.
But, if you mean happy as in 'everything is okay',
Like before,
Then, no,
I could never write that way
For you or anyone else;
The world has changed forever -
Don't you realize that by now?-
But, how could you,
Not being one of 'those people' afflicted with tragedy?
I know how it is...
I used to shake my head at the sad news stories
Of 'those people', too,
Before changing the channel
And grabbing a fistful of popcorn.

*D*ecember 10, 2009

Now the final memorial of this year has come
When I stare at the brass-framed portraits of my sons
Trumpeting more loudly of heaven
Than the too-obvious miracle of life
Taken back so early.
Laid to rest one year ago today,
These medalled sons in honor lie
Behind well-attended flowers
Speaking of love and life
Beyond the marble-fronted crypt,
And in hearts refusing and unable to forget.
What matters the length of life,
But that it be worthy of glory?
And then a glance to the left
Contrasts my own bare crypt
Awaiting name and photograph,
And the number of my years
With space enough for marks of love,
Respect and honor, too, (if so deserved).
Unlike Scrooge, I see no horror
In my family name displayed above my sons',
Nor in the blank marble slate
Awaiting what shall be written there;
No, not horror,
But incentive, caution, alertness,
Even invitation, encouragement and beckoning love.
That blank marble slate
Could just as well be a curtained window
Closed to the glorious vision of heaven
Until the Lord decide the time it should be opened.
One day my body, too, shall lie entombed,
Though less tragically, beside my sons,
For it is more 'normal' for adults to die;

And hopefully the closeness of our crypts
Will witness to our unity in heaven.
Until then, the liturgical year with its feasts and seasons
Shall be interspersed with memorials of my sons
Reminding me to keep my eyes on Jesus,
Who alone gives life its meaning and true direction.

This Advent of good news

On the third Sunday of Advent
The Prophet Isaiah said,
"With joy you shall draw water
From the wells of salvation!"
And from within my rock-walled heart
I looked up into the eyes of the Lord and understood:
My heart had never been -
Was never meant to be -
A canyon.
Hewn by the pain of my sons' deaths,
The Lord had carved a reservoir,
And rushed in with His healing balm
Of love and peace,
And joy flowing to the brim -
Though the pain of absence yet remains -
That my life might be filled with His life;
And, peering at my pregnant wife,
My joy overflows in tears
For the wondrous gift within her once again.
Deep within the reservoir of my heart,
The Lord walks upon the waters,
And with Him, hand-in-hand,
My little sons who've gone before
Dance and splash with joy
For the gift of life
Tabernacled in their mother's womb,
Their joy rippling through my heart and soul,
Through my lifelong Advent
Anticipating the coming of the Lord
Each Christmas and at the end of time;
Through this Advent of good news
Of a new birth in a new year;
Another child to present to the Father;
Another child already loved.

Guardian of the sacred

When I raise my soul in prayer
For my little family, Lord,
I bear them on my back
As though with eagle's wings
To carry them to Your throne;
Yet, this image is from You,
Telling me for fathers this is so
By the very fact of fatherhood
And marriage in Your sight,
And this strength is my right
Through the sacrament's great power.
I stand as the guardian of the sacred
In our domestic church, our home,
My wife its gentle beating heart,
Our children born as gifts from the Father
Entrusting them to our care
That they might choose the Lord in love
And turn to Him in prayer.
Lift my arms in battle, Lord!
Though the enemy crowd the very door,
Let me bear my family safe in prayer,
Your angels on either side,
And my two sons who've gone before,
To steady my trembling arms like Moses
Assisted by the Hebrews long ago,
Unyielding before their foes;
Strengthen me in the lengthening fight
That I not rest until You decide
When the war for me shall end,
Yet certain the final victory is Yours.

The miracle of you

Come, Little One,
In health and peace and happiness
To bless the world
With a plan given no other.
What has He willed for you?
All in good time;
All in His time, my child;
God shall make it known.
May His will bring you safely to your birth
And fill my heart with canticles of love,
My arms with the miracle of you.
Just one week until Christmas -
Though your birth shall be months after His -
May you be filled with grace
When the Presence of the Lord
Fills the heart and soul of your mother
Receiving Him in the Eucharist,
And you partaking of all that she consumes
By dispensation of the womb.
O, Little One,
Know that I love you
Though you be unaware of my existence
In your universe in utero.
Looking to the heavens
From the womb of my little world,
I realize the Father says the same to me
So often introspective and unaware
As He awaits my birth into eternal life.
How great must be the Father's love
If my heart, aching for my sons who've gone before,
And for you just newly conceived,
Be a mere reflection of His love;
Would He not gather us immediately to His heart
If not for having given us free will,
And having to wait for us to choose?
How spectacular must the free choice be
Of a soul to love the Father;

For the desire of every father
Is for his child to love him,
And for his child to know he is loved...
As I love you.

$\mathcal{P}$ilgrimage

How wonderful it would be
To sit on the hill where Jesus taught;
To gaze across those shimmering vistas
And recite the Beatitudes
On the very spot they were first spoken by the Lord.
What powerful emotions would arise
If I could stand beneath the dome of St. Peter's,
Climb the road to Monte Cassino
Built by the holy founder St. Benedict,
Kneel before the tombs of Sts. Damien of Molokai,
Padre Pio and Bernadette Soubirous,
Pray the rosary at Fatima,
Stare lovingly at the image of Our Lady of Guadalupe
On the tilma of St. Juan Diego,
Or view the shrine to St. Joseph built
By the prayers of Blessed André of Montreal.
How wonderful it would be...
One day it could be, God willing;
Until then, my humble pilgrimage
Finds its culmination before the Eucharistic Lord
Hidden in His tiny chapel;
Before the same Lord
Who spoke the Beatitudes so long ago
And still today;
Before the same Lord
Who inspired the faith in all the saints
Giving their lives in service
Encouraging others to do the same.
All that those others lived for, strived for, suffered for, died for...
This Jesus,
Reigns from this simple monstrance,
As in all the famous shrines around the world,
Though without the same glory,
Or history of signs and wonders.
From Bethlehem to St. Peter's...

Did not all the famous Christian places begin that way
Until Jesus came with the light of Faith?
And nothing could ever stay the same.
How wonderful it is!

Come to save the world

The Midnight Mass in St. Peter's ends,
And here it is but 3 PM,
The hour of mercy before the Birthday of the Lord.
We yet have time to call on Him:
Have mercy, Lord!
We are not worthy that You should come;
Depart from us, for we are sinful...
No, stay!
For who else could save us,
If not You?
O, Merciful Savior!
You come as a mere Babe,
Defenseless and innocent,
Drawing the most hardened to reach for You
And cradle You to his chest
Where Your heart might speak to his;
Now the Source of joy is known,
And unburdened hearts might overflow
In tear-choked glorias
Angelic in the soul's release;
And all creation begins anew
When seen through the eyes of grace,
For all is Yours, as are we
Subject to You, O Mighty King,
Come humbly to take Your throne
In each heart falling in adoration
Before You born a helpless baby
To conquer with such simple love
That cannot be denied.
You came for us!
To die for us!
O, gentle Lamb!
If it should ease Your journey to the cross;
If it should lighten the cross' weight,

Take my heart for Your throne!
Let me be for You like Lazarus, Your friend,
Who loved You to the grave,
And believed You to be the Resurrection and the Life,
Come to save the world!

Safekeeping

Let me place my hand upon your belly,
Just above your womb,
That I might reach out to our child within
Through nurturing warmth whispering patience
Until the time of growth has passed;
Soon your hands by subconscious command
Shall caress our child through your swollen belly,
Your maternal heart singing lullabies
Beneath the sound of your own hearing.
I shall laugh at the vigorous thump of indignant limbs
At unwanted pressure on a shrinking world;
Shall laugh discreetly at your feigned injuries,
Half-proud for the strength of our child
Displayed against your belly from within.

Come into this living,
This existence given by God!
O, child! I shall not fear for you...
Shall try not to fear for you;
How I long to gaze enraptured at your innocence,
Feel the furious force of paternal love
Swell my inadequate heart
In truth dependent on the grace of God.

I am not worthy, Lord,
That You should bless me with another child;
Yet, I lovingly accept this gift bestowed
In trust and our safe-keeping...
For as long a time as You decree;
I shall praise You in the Now beneath my fingertips,
For another soul exists to glorify You
Here, and for all eternity.

The tongue

How nice it is to know of you,
To speak through emails
With filtered words weighed carefully
That my inner meaning might be clear;
I fear (through past experience),
If one day we speak face-to-face,
I may allow my tongue the freedom
It does not deserve,
And words may be spoken
Which might not have been
Had I been more vigilant.
Words uttered carelessly in jest,
When misunderstood, often wound,
Cause scandal or division
When no harm had ever been intended.
Once done, though,
How difficult it is to mend!

The tongue must be leashed
Like a half-trained dog learning to heel;
Unchecked, it often leaps up,
Offending those nearby
With unwanted dirt or effusive affection,
Its owner shamed and mortified
At the lack of discipline displayed
While the one soiled walks away
Thinking twice about coming back that way again.

*C*ome forth – a meditation

The two old women knelt on either side of the elderly man, each clutching one of his hands to their lips, then caressing them to tear-wetted cheeks. They smiled at him. He rested peacefully against his pillows, his skin translucent as though he had already begun the final journey. He was ready now. He tried to keep his sisters in focus, tried to smile to let them know he was comfortable; he had lost the power of speech just hours ago, and now it seemed his eyes were failing him also. No matter. He had said his goodbyes to his wife and children standing nearby. His sisters had been the last to arrive. He was glad they were in time; he knew how upset they would have been to arrive too late. Well, at any rate, they had already seen him die once, he chuckled to himself. How different that had been! He had been so young, so healthy when the sickness took hold and ravaged his body so quickly there had been no time for help to arrive. How differently he had lived his second life; no, not differently... better. Had he really lived another fifty years? It seemed like a blur: the celebration of being alive again, his wedding, the birth of his firstborn, his work, more children... through it all, the love of his good wife, and his faith; yes, most of all, his faith.

Already the light was growing dimmer, the gentle sounds of weeping more muffled. Yet, he began to see reality more clearly – the purpose of all 'things'. Of course, He was there; He had always been there, by faith, and at last He was coming into sight. Ah, yes, it was Him for certain, but... more than he remembered. "Goodbye," he called, though his lips never moved; he squeezed his sisters' hands, though they felt no pressure.

He had learned in life that creation speaks of God. Death and resurrection were reflected everywhere, if one only looked. The year ends, another begins; seeds are planted, crops harvested; the sun rises, then sets. Earthly life trumpets life in God. Every moment becomes a conscious act of awareness of the Presence of God.

He wondered why he should think such thoughts now, at the end. The room had disappeared from his sight, though he was aware of it. Another light had begun to grow around him, though he was puzzled, since, in this light, the other did not deserve to be called 'light'. He felt no fear, only increasing peace and joy... a longing being fulfilled.

What had he been thinking about? Oh, yes, the Presence of God. Life, and the grace of God, had taught him to reduce all reminders of the divine to the simplest reflection: breathing. Inhale; Come Holy Spirit! Exhale; Lord Jesus, have mercy! Breathe in and out; love-mercy, love-mercy.

The light shone brilliantly. It was not a thing, but a Person. "I know You," he thought, reaching out.

"I know you, too, Lazarus," said the Master. "Come forth!"

Lazarus inhaled one last time, entering completely into the Presence of God.

$\mathcal{G}$lory made manifest

Though hidden in the Virgin's womb,
Your glory was made manifest
At the exclamation of Elizabeth
(Made young by the fruitfulness of her womb)
When she heard the greeting of Your Mother
Even before the Source of grace drew near;
And by Your cousin's dance in utero -
So eager was he to tell the world -
That one meeting would have been enough
To sustain him through the desert's trials
And the falling sword of Herod,
For he came to birth with You enshrined
As Our Lady nursed his mother
Through those ninety days of adoration.

Your glory was made manifest
In Gospel accounts for all to read
The prophecies fulfilled;
And now the case before us is:
Bow down or walk away.

Must the star above the manger,
Or the angels arrayed in glory,
Or the magi bearing gifts
Be the only ways convincing us
You, indeed, are God?
For, once convinced by what others wrote,
Have we not in our own lives
Epiphanies to share?

Your glory, Lord, is made manifest
In the grace Your sacraments bestow:
Your Life becomes our life,
Your Father becomes our own;
Your glory is made manifest
In lives made manifestations of You.

$\mathcal{B}$eatitude

O Little One,
I held you in my heart
Wounded with love at the expectation of you.
My arms now cradle your stricken mother,
Hopes of another infant
Washed away in tearful laments
Cast heart-flung at tabernacle walls;
I wanted you!
I want you!
While the last shred of hope survives
Swaddling you in your mother's womb;
(Can God's grace not defy the odds against you?)
I want the growing anticipation of you
To come back,
Your mother's eyes pregnant with hopes of seeing you,
Not another year draped in the shadows of death;
Must we have more children in heaven
Than nestled in our home?

O God!

I... will... submit, Lord,
My hand stretched out to You...
At You...
My fingers opening,
Pleading,
Putting away my clenched fist
With the belief
Heaven will hold my Little One
And...
Blessed are those who mourn.

The offering of my lament

My tears praise You, O God,
And my trembling lips
Mouth silent words: Thy will be done,
As the fires of my burning heart
Flare again at this death of my Little One.
I have no coffin to have carried in,
No body to cradle even one first time,
No features to remember from this day on -
No memories of this child at all -
Save only the knowledge of conception,
And then... demise.
I wrote before of acceptance
For as long a time as You decreed...
And, I do accept, Lord,
But, it is so hard
To bury newborn hopes and joy
Swirling like swallows thrilled to be alive,
Especially with what went... before.

Were we not worthy, Lord?

Or, do You think us able
To bear this burden, too?

How You have blessed this child
Awakened to eternity
With original sin washed away
In a baptism of desire
Burning in our hearts for this baby's birth, too,
But which was not meant to be;
Such purity surely must please You, Lord,
So take this child, as is Your right,
To play before Your throne;
And take the offering of my lament

In this Year of the Priest
And bless all priests in Your service
With faithful, fruitful ministry
Bringing many souls to You
In memory of my Little One.

Your soul ecstatic

We were joyful... then,
Not knowing you were gone;
And now I know, my heart-borne child,
You slipped away before the New Year's birth,
And we toasting it thought pregnant with life
When the old had marred its end with sorrow,
Our hopes hollow in the echoes of an empty womb.

Into the arms of my sons who've gone before,
Rise, Little One, created for eternity!
No stain shall ever touch you,
Not even the overprotective love of your father,
Or the insatiable love of your mother;
Yet our longing for your birth
Desired your being born a child of God, too,
And, freed from original sin,
And having known no other reality,
Your awareness dawned in the Beatific Vision
With the knowledge of our souls' saving desire,
And your soul ecstatic with joy.

O magnificent leap from death to life
With no earthly sorrow hindering
And no sad earthly lingering!

I will bear the temporary loss of you
That you be found in the arms of God;
I will release my presumption of your birth
Before the unclouded wisdom of God;
I wll quiet the storms of mere emotion
And rouse the fires of faith to see
Another child of mine a saint with God!

$\mathcal{H}$is Cross through my cross

Lay but this day's cross upon me
For yesterday's has strengthened me for today
And tomorrow's is too heavy yet to bear.
Lay me, crucified, upon the palm of my Father
Bearing me upward to gaze upon me with love;
He takes me for His son for His Son's sake.
Let me rest in the throes my Father sends
Rather than search on my own as though
A better way to heaven could be found;
For beautiful in its consequence is pain
When mingled with self-sacrifice
Opening the heart to Christian paradox:
Love finds joy in suffering for the Lord;
His Cross through my cross brings grace;
His Love through my love, His Face.

An answer to their prayers

I thought because two sons died through another's fault
I could claim the Third World poor as brothers;
For are not starvation and war injustice, too,
Stealing the lives of countless children
Even as their mothers cradle them in the dust,
Dry as the hopes in their wasted eyes?
Have I not been blessed enough in life, though,
That I must claim their suffering, too -
That which cries out to God on their behalf
For the crimes against them:
Greed, corruption... and apathy?
Perhaps the sudden death of my sons
May open my eyes
To see how comfortable my life has been -
Even as I mourned -
And the Third World poor are indeed my brothers
Calling out to God our Father,
And I am meant to be
An answer to their prayers.

*M*editation on the Feast of the Conversion of

St. Paul January 25

We live in our own certainties -
They may be true or false -
But even if those certainties be true,
Pride in them may make us worse
Than if certainties though false were humbly lived.

Strike me from the steed of pride, Lord!
Lay me in the dust with blinded eyes
That I must call for help
And clutch the graces sent to guide me
Lest I fall again unable to rise
From the darkness of my own choosing.

Once cast down,
Peel the scales covering my eyes;
Reveal the nothingness of my own strength
And I shall see truly for the first time
How beautiful it is
To be always looking up with raised arms
As an infant reaching for his Father.

The world may do what it will;
What is that in the light of Your grace?
All suffering, striving, living are for You,
Who saves from every false "certainty";
And from the vantage of humility,
Clothed in the undefeatable armor of Your love,
I shall speak the truth that Jesus is God,
Even as the sword blow falls.

$\mathcal{M}$editation on the Feast of the Presentation

February 2

I was there, in the mind of the Saviour,
As were you,
When, as a child,
He was presented to the Father
In the temple in Jerusalem;
For He is God,
And, though borne in the arms of Simeon
Two thousand years ago,
He thought of all then who ever lived,
And thinks of all now who ever shall,
And keeps us in existence
In spite of the iniquities
He came to bear as though His own.
No wonder Simeon rejoiced
To hold Redemption in his hands!
"Now let Your servant die in peace," he prayed,
For what more was there to see
With the promise of the Lord fulfilled?
He foretold the cross to come
As he handed back the Child
Into your arms, O Virgin Mother,
And foretold your steps would follow closely His.
He wept to gaze into your eyes,
For it was for Simeon, too, the Lord would die...
And for all of us
That the awful price be paid for Adam's sin
Closing heaven until He came!
And did you weep as though to say,
"He shall die for me, His Mother, too,
That all might be children of the Father."?
Yet, even knowing this, you took the Lord
And presented Him to God.
Did you see the shadow of His cross upon the altar
And you whispering, "I love You, Lord,"

As the Levite held Him there aloft,
Lifting God to God?
And when out beneath the bright Jerusalem sky,
As you kissed the Infant Saviour in your arms,
Did you love Him more... knowing He would die?

Two sons of mine were killed, too, dear Mother,
Though I, of course, was mercifully unaware
Of how much time I had to hold them close,
For I could not have borne the knowledge of their approaching
death
While they yet filled my home with joy -
It is hard enough to bear it even now.

I, too, presented my children to the Lord,
brought my sons as babes to the baptismal font,
The priest lifting them from the rippled pool
With the trinitarian words newly spoken...
They became sons of God
Through the suffering and death of Jesus,
Their cross implicit in the sacrament's saving grace;
But...
To be crucified so young...
Rather, we parents are the crucified;
Their death became our cross
Made lighter, though,
By faith in the sacrament's other truth in their regard:
Resurrection...
To be glorified so young!

Mother,
Did you miss the presence of Your Son -
The way He looked and talked and smiled at you -
After He ascended to the Father?
It helps to think you did,
To believe you understand
The ever-present ache I have for my sons
As once I knew them here.

Send my love to them!

And speak to me more of faith and hope and love
Now and at the hour of my death.

AFTERWORD

Thank-you dear reader, for joining me on my journey of
mourning, at its beginning at least; for, when you finish this little
book, and perhaps return to it sometimes, you will, of course,
continue the path of your own life, hopefully with renewed
appreciation for its blessings. While my wife and I naturally shall
mourn for the rest of our lives, we intend to live with as much
joy as possible. This may seem a contradiction, yet I believe it is
not, for if we were to remain bound by grief we would be blinded
to life's goodness; mourning recognizes blessings in spite of pain;
it encompasses grief, envelopes it and builds on it as a grain of
sand in an oyster becomes a precious pearl, which would never
have existed had the pain of that grain of sand not been there
first.

I wish to thank for their support my wife and sons journeying
with me and whose love helps keep me going, relatives and
friends who suggested I submit my writing for publication, my
close friend Fr. Ian Stuart for years of spiritual encouragement
and for writing the book's foreward, Mr. Michael D. O'Brien for
taking the time to read this book and for his gracious comments
provided for its promotion, Ms. Michelle Halket for publishing it
and making the whole process simple, and everyone who
purchased and read All In God's Time, My Sons.

God bless.

Geoff Moeller
Feast of the Presentation of the Lord
February 2, 2010

ABOUT THE AUTHOR

Geoff Moeller was born in the arctic and lived in towns across Canada's north and west, but grew up in the Fraser Valley of British Columbia. He completed high school at the Seminary of Christ the King under the guidance of the Benedictines of Westminster Abbey in Mission, BC, then spent several years as a member of the community as well. Geoff also credits the monks with the solid foundation he received in the Catholic Faith passed on from his parents. A Benedictine at heart, he is an oblate of Westminster Abbey. He presently works for Metro Vancouver Regional Parks. He lives in Vancouver with his wife Maria and their sons Karl and Lorenzo.

Breinigsville, PA USA
19 April 2010
236454BV00001B/1/P